HOW TO SURVIVE THE LOSS OF A CHILD

Filling the Emptiness and Rebuilding Your Life

Catherine M. Sanders, Ph.D.

Prima Publishing
P.O. Box 1260
Rocklin, CA 95677

Copyediting by Toni Murray
Production by Janelle Rohr, Bookman Productions
Typography by AeroType, Inc.
Interior design by Judith Levinson
Cover design by The Dunlavey Studio

Library of Congress Cataloging-in-Publication Data

Sanders, Catherine M.
    How to survive the loss of a child : filling the emptiness and rebuilding your life / by Catherine Sanders.
      p. cm.
    Includes index.
    ISBN 1-55958-164-6 : $18.95
    1. Bereavement—Psychological aspects. 2. Grief. 3. Loss (Psychology) I. Title
    BF575.G7S27 1992
    155.9'37—dc20   91-39327
                                        CIP

94 95 96 97 RRD 10 9 8 7 6 5 4 3 2 1

Printed in the United States of America

How to Order:
Quantity discounts are available from the publisher, Prima Publishing, P.O. Box 1260SAN, Rocklin, CA 95677; telephone (916) 632-7400. On your letterhead, include information concerning the intended use of the books and the number of books you wish to purchase.

*I dedicate this book in loving memory
to my mother,
the one who gave me life,
Alma Jane Petty Alling,
and
to my son,
the one to whom I gave life,
James William Sanders.*

*I will always cherish
the precious memories
of our time together.*

Contents

Acknowledgments

First and foremost, I want to acknowledge the tremendous help and input of my daughter, Catherine O. Merrill. As a professor of English at Johnson State College in Johnson, Vermont, she is eternally busy with her share of student papers to edit. Even with this, she found time to edit each chapter of my book and offer critical comments that were invaluable. Catherine has been one of my most ardent supporters; she gave me worlds of strength and encouragement. How wonderful to have a child grow up and be a professional cohort.

Too, I am especially grateful to my dear friend Mary Howren Howerton, who gave so generously of her time to read the manuscript (even rereading some chapters several times), looking for typos and other mistakes. She offered many positive suggestions that helped clear the cobwebs from both my writing and my brain.

Thanks go to my friend and office sidekick, Kay Burns, who typed endless notes and corrections to the manuscript, always struggling to read my hastily prepared changes; to Martha and Cecil Clark and Marlene and Dick Ashman of Compassionate Friends of Charlotte, who supplied important information; and to Kelly Hamilton of Kinder-Mourn, Inc. of Charlotte, for her insight into funeral rituals for tiny infants.

Special thanks also go to my agent, Julie Castiglia, of Waterside Productions, Inc. in Del Mar, California. Julie was the one who encouraged me to write this book in the first place. I am indebted to Jennifer Basye of

Prima Publishing. She has been most understanding and patient in extending deadlines, and her support helped so much throughout the writing of this book.

My deepest appreciation goes to Janelle Rohr of Bookman Productions, who moved this book smoothly and painlessly (for me, anyhow) through the production phase to its final form.

Sincerest thanks are offered to Toni Murray, who provided development and copyediting. Her suggestions and comments were invaluable. She did a wonderful job, and I am eternally grateful.

To my friend and editor of my two earlier books, Herb Reich, at John Wiley & Sons, Inc., I express my appreciation for his interest and encouragement in the writing of this book. He knew how important it was to me.

I want to express my deepest appreciation to Cynthia Carlson and Bill Bullock, two wonderful friends, who supplied constant encouragement during the long months of writing. Our "silent retreats" in the mountains were regenerating for us all.

I would be remiss if I did not mention the loving support I received from my sister, Mary Mckinney, and from my two other daughters, Sue Labella and Sally Bowers. Their nurturance and love sustained me all through the writing of the book.

Ultimately, however, my deepest gratitude goes to the wonderful families in the Tampa Bereavement Study who shared their feelings at a time when their hearts were breaking. Their hopes were that what they could offer would ease the way for other bereaved parents. Their wonderful generosity and loving compassion form the real basis for this book.

Catherine M. Sanders

Introduction

The death of a child is an impossible grief. In a culture that values youth above all, the death of a child is viewed as the greatest of all tragedies. The impossibility of surviving one's child is foremost in the thoughts of bereaved parents, and the question of Why? is an obsessive rumination. Families and friends are at a loss as to what to say or how to help. Everyone becomes paralyzed. Would-be supporters find it easier to stay away.

This is the most difficult book I have ever written, yet for me the most important. With this book, I feel that I have come full circle. My experience with grief began when my son, Jim, was killed in a waterskiing accident. After searching the literature for information that could help me deal with this loss, I came up practically empty-handed. At that time, more emphasis was placed on the dying person than the grieving survivor.

It took several years before I could bring myself to begin a research project on grief. Simply surviving was the most I could manage. At that time not only were there few books on grief, but in my area there were no support groups to join—no place to offer answers to the blind questions I flung out.

My struggle eventually led me to design and carry out the Tampa Bereavement Study. The study was a research project implemented to learn more about the effects of grief following the death of a parent, spouse, or child. If I could determine which grief caused the most severe reaction, intervention strategies could be devised to help the bereaved survivors who needed help the most. During the project, I interviewed 120 bereaved people shortly after the death of a significant person. In the majority of cases, I followed each survivor through the first two years of bereavement. The death of a child ranked overwhelmingly as the most significant loss anyone can ever experience. Since that time, this finding has been corroborated in countless studies.

The initial purpose of my study was to learn what caused the awful pain, the physical gut-wrenching pain of grief. I eventually learned that the pain cannot be circumvented. It must be borne in its full vengeance, with awareness. What can help, however, is to understand as much as possible about grief even before it happens. That way, we can, at least, know what to expect.

Helping bereaved parents and family members survive one of the bleakest periods of their lives is the major focus of this book. Understanding the symptoms and the process of grief is important in that it helps reduce the fear of losing control over one's life forever. But equally important, one needs to have the assurance that life will once again offer some sense of joy and peace, that the agonizing pain will someday diminish.

This book deals with the five phases of bereavement: shock, awareness of loss, conservation/withdrawal, healing, and renewal. It describes the symptoms—physical, emotional, and social—that one can expect to experience. Knowing the normal course of grief can be extremely helpful to the bereaved. Not only can they determine where they are in the grief process, but they can understand the normality of the symptoms they are experiencing.

Studies show that marital discord, separation, and divorce are common after a child's death. Just at a time when family members most need mutual support and understanding, they feel the greatest degree of familial disharmony. The shock that serves to protect survivors from raw pain in early stages of grief also serves to isolate them from each other's pain. Besides this, family members do not grieve alike. Mothers see the child differently from fathers. Siblings, grandparents, and extended family members have different perspectives on what they have lost. Each of these losses must be acknowledged and dealt with as seriously and attentively as the next one.

This book also addresses special cases of unacknowledged bereavement: miscarriage, stillbirth, and induced abortion. Too often, society fails to legitimize grief from these losses. As a result, the bereaved parents do not receive critically needed support and patient understanding.

In most cases of bereavement, the shock phase is over in the first few weeks after the loss. Not so in parental grief. The death of a child takes much longer to process, because the factors involved are compounded. Guilt and anger keep grief alive long past the time other forms of bereavement are resolved. The parent-child bond must be relinquished. When the child dies, the parents grieve not only for the deprivation of being without their child, but also for lost aspects of themselves. Identification is experienced so personally that parents often report actually feeling the impact that killed their child or suffering the pain that accompanied the fatal illness. In addition, their child provided a future with hopes, dreams, and aspirations. With their child's death, their own immortality has been thwarted, their future interrupted or stolen.

Yet it is experiencing grief, not denying or escaping it, that finally heals us. When we actively move through the phases of grief, we are working toward restoration. Understanding these phases, knowing what to expect and—most importantly—learning that there are some things we can do to help ourselves, can give us greater assurance of the normality of our grief. Because parental grief takes so long to resolve, it often feels like a chronic state that will last forever. Reassurances that we are moving through a normal process, not stagnating, can help reduce much of the debilitating stress of bereavement.

Through my own research, through clinical work with bereaved parents, and through my own personal experience, I have drawn from a wide variety of resources. The names and identities of the persons whose stories are told in this book have been changed to protect their anonymity and the confidentiality of their disclosures. Circumstances have been slightly altered for the same reasons. The bereaved parents who contributed to this work shared their stories in the hope that by doing so they would be able to help other grieving parents. I am eternally grateful for their trust and their thoughtful generosity in sharing their lives.

My ultimate wish in writing this book is to help promote understanding of the process of grief; to offer suggestions for recovery; and to reassure the bereaved that, through all their intense suffering, they will survive and, in time, feel joy and peace once more.

1

• • • • • • • • • • • • • • • •

The Ultimate Tragedy

I CAN'T *remember how it started...it was just a dream, but I was talking to Maggie and she asked me how she died. And I told her what happened...I explained to her just like I always explained a lot of things—all the way from where the sun rises and all of that stuff—I just went ahead and explained it. "Well, you fell into the pool and drowned." And then she said, "Oh, now I understand. Can I come back?" And I said, "Well, no, you can't." It was like, "Well, now I understand what happened, then is it okay if I come back." And I had to say no. When I woke, I felt awful—like I really had rejected her. It really choked me up. It would have been so good if I could have said Yes, you can come back.*

—Bereaved father, age 28

Bereavement following the death of a child is more intense than any other form of grief. The pain is like an open sore that fails to heal. Time and time again a temporary scar forms, only to break open again with no warning. The agonizing intensity of the hurt rocks the very depths of our being, and we feel as if we will be permanently damaged and emotionally dislodged by this tragic event. We are afraid we will never fully recover. Yet—we learn to survive. We learn to move on into a strange new life until we can finally come to terms with a different world. Things are never the same. We have come to see that life is temporary and that we have no real control. The dreams of the past have hardened, solidified. We have buried our innocence.

Once upon a time I believed that there was a natural progression in life. I believed that just as in all of nature, we grew to maturity, produced our offspring, and eventually died. Our children's lives then followed the same progression. The cycle of life was perpetuated and our lineage guaranteed.

Now, I know better. I wonder at my early naïveté. Hadn't I heard that children could die? Could I have read about it and heard about it but denied the possibility? Or did I believe it could only happen to someone else, not to me? Before my son was killed, the thought that one of my children could die had never seriously entered my mind.

In our culture the death of a young child is actually a rare event. Once a child hits adolescence, however, the chance of death increases considerably, primarily because of accidents. Automobiles account for a large percentage of the deaths of adolescents. Teenagers are adventurous, feel that they are invincible, and simply take a lot of chances.

Whatever the child's age, if the child dies, the parent suffers. Learning of the death feels like a blow to the stomach. You can't breathe or move. The unexpectedness is more than anyone can comprehend.

The day of a tragedy usually begins quite normally for most. We get up, brush our teeth, put on some make-up if we're women, shave if we're men, decide what to wear. We eat breakfast, or maybe not. In retrospect, the incomprehensible thing about the day is its sameness. But before the day is over, events take place that are irreversible. Everything is changed forever. Someone we love has been taken from us—a child is irretrievably gone.

So many holidays begin and end this way. Memorial Day, the Fourth of July or—as it was for us—Labor Day. In our desire to celebrate the occasion, we become careless. We become momentarily distracted and, when we turn our backs for a moment, it happens.

We took precautions that Labor Day to stay off the highway. We chose to remain at home and enjoy our new waterfront Florida home, where we would be safe. Why leave? We had everything we needed right there to enjoy ourselves: a swimming pool, our own dock, a ski boat.

Jim, our son, especially liked the boat and spent most of his time taking it out, skiing, and visiting new friends who also had waterfront homes. Our dock had become a gathering place for teenagers, and I loved to see Jim enjoying himself with his new friends. He had always been a shy kid, so the move from Massachusetts had been a difficult adjustment. He had only recently met a group of boys that he felt comfortable with.

Jim loved to build model airplanes or reconstruct engines of any kind. He was also an avid reader. He had never been an athlete. His poor eyesight kept him out of most sports. Since we had been in Florida, though, Jim had become an excellent water-skier. For the first time in his life, he felt competent at a sport. He didn't need perfect eyesight to ski, or so we thought. In the end, however, his blurred vision probably caused his death.

Since our move from Massachusetts to Florida, Jim had been having a tough time in school. He failed algebra in his first term there. His failure was hard to understand because he had placed in the 99th percentile in mathematics in the National Merit exams the year before. He seemed to be having trouble adjusting to what was for him a new type of school environment. In Massachusetts, he had been attending a small private school where he felt comfortable and at home. Now he was going to the large public high school in St. Petersburg. Besides, we had moved in the middle of the year—a hard situation for most kids in any case.

Just to motivate him, I decided to take some courses at the local junior college. Maybe if he saw me working hard, he would be encouraged. My classes had started only the week before.

That day, when Jim came down to breakfast midmorning, I was studying my French. I remember he made some very funny comments about my courses, and we laughed at my rudimentary French pronunciations.

It was a leisurely day for us all. Catherine, our youngest daughter, had a friend over and was playing in the pool. Hersh, my husband, was relaxing with a book. Routine. Nothing much happening.

A little after noon, Jim said he was going water skiing with his friends. I asked him to be home by 3:30 because we wanted to have the boat for a while later in the day.

Watching him walk down to the dock, I thought how well he was filling out. He was tall, his shoulders broadening. And a really nice guy. I remember thinking how proud of him I was.

Jim left our dock, the boat making a wide sweep across the green bay. Then he was out of sight. That was the last time I saw him alive.

A little after 3:00, I was lying by the pool when I saw a powerboat speeding toward the dock. It wasn't our boat.

Jim's best friend, Ken, was standing in the bow. As soon as he saw me, he screamed, "Get an ambulance—Jim's been hurt!" Hersh tore down to the dock. I ran to the phone to call the rescue squad. I gave the squad directions, and I ran back toward the boat. But Hersh yelled for me to get help from the neighbors a block down the street. I still hadn't seen Jim. I didn't know that Hersh had sent me away just so I wouldn't see how badly our son was hurt.

Who knows how long it took the ambulance to arrive. I don't think it was long, but I could never tell now. It seemed forever. In the confusion, my jumbled, racing mind was like a fast-changing kaleidoscope, one perception flashing on the next before I even knew what to make of the last one. The terror I felt clawed at my heart. I could hardly breathe.

The rescue squad worked on Jim for an hour and finally got him breathing. (I didn't know he hadn't been.) His color was coming back. We gave a long sigh of relief. He wasn't conscious, but he would be all right now, we felt sure. How our denial systems work at these times. We didn't know that the breathing was only artificially induced and that the return of color was from the oxygen he was receiving. We didn't know that Jim had suffered a cerebral hemorrhage and a broken neck when he had been hit by an oncoming boat.

Jim was put into the ambulance. Hersh and I followed in our car, but we lost the squad on the way. We arrived at the hospital a few minutes after the ambulance. Dashing in, we rushed to the emergency-room desk and asked to see our son. The nurse asked us to wait in a small examining room down the hall. On the way, I caught sight of the rescue squad members who had been at our house. They were somber, not making eye contact. My heart froze again.

I don't know how long we waited before the doctor came in. I jumped up, asking how Jim was. Without a moment's hesitation or preparation, the doctor said, "Your son is dead!"

The world stopped. All I can remember of that moment is turning inward—closing the world out. I sat frozen. There was no show of emotion. I simply couldn't make my outside world match my inner one.

The doctor left. A nurse came in and asked, "Why don't you cry?" I was still motionless. Too numb to answer. Too numb to care to answer. A life was over, but I couldn't understand even what that meant. It would take years for me to understand that I could never understand.

We pieced the accident together later. It was one of those freak situations where a second either way could have saved him. Jim was skiing behind our boat while a boatful of friends was coming in the opposite direction. Jim swung out wide but apparently didn't calculate his distance correctly, not realizing that the boat was as close as it was. When he got near enough to see, it was too late. Dropping the rope, he sank into the water. The other boat apparently didn't have time to turn and barreled into him. The impact was so hard that it knocked the driver out of the other boat.

We left the hospital that day, a pitiful couple with a small bundle of clothing in a paper bag. Our son, gone.

WE HAVE A SPECIAL BOND WITH OUR CHILDREN

Our connection to our children is a unique relationship. We are tied to our children by a strong bond that is more than one of blood. There are connections that represent not only our own need to belong as a part of a family unit, but also a need to have a part of ourselves passed along to future generations.

Our children become a part of us not only because they

are our flesh and blood, but for many other reasons. Our emotional ties are strong. We see ourselves in them. We search their features, body types, and even behavior to catch a small likeness of ourselves. When we find similarities, we feel a sense of connectedness and pride.

Our children are love objects for us. In addition, our love for our mate is heightened by the common concern parents have for their children. We feel more connected as mates because our love as a couple is shared with them. Then to complete the circle, that love is returned to us in full measure by our children.

When we have children, we have passed a societal landmark. Parenthood is a coming of age. If we were treated as young and inexperienced before, now others may view us as adults with adult responsibilities. We receive more authority and power, rights, and privileges. People take us more seriously.

Joe and Sarah were only nineteen when they married and had their first child. Joe hadn't attended college but had jumped directly from high school into the world of men and work. Life was okay. Then their little girl drowned one Fourth of July. In an unsupervised moment the 2½-year-old had wandered into the lake. Although she was rescued quickly, the rescue wasn't fast enough to save her life. Later, Joe talked with me about all the things his daughter had meant to him.

Besides being such a joyful little person, really lighting up our lives, she gave me something else. You see, before she was born, I had always felt so young around the guys at work...you know...real inexperienced about life and all that. Well, when Cindy was born, they suddenly started treating me different...more like one of them. I thought maybe just being a father made me look more grown up. It must have been that, else they wouldn't have treated me any different from what they did before.

Part of the unique bond Joe had with his daughter was due to the privilege fatherhood provided him in his work world. When the bond was broken, it was as if that privilege were taken back again.

WE IDENTIFY WITH OUR CHILDREN

Our identification with our children is not only because they look or act like us, but that in raising them we share such a large part of life with them. We habituate to our children. We see their foibles, their vulnerable side, their idiosyncrasies. We nurse them through their sicknesses. We comfort them when they are afraid. As our children develop and grow, so does our personal involvement.

Through our close ties, our children become a part of us and we see our own child selves in them. Their childhood years become a reliving of our own childhoods. As this happens, we see ourselves in them even more. When they die, we lose an enormous chunk of ourselves.

When Jimmy died, I believe my own child self died as well, for I could feel that playful part of me closing off. For twenty-eight years I involved myself in very grown-up pursuits and seemingly forgot my child self. First, I worked toward and received my Ph.D.—a real grown-up thing to do. After that, I focused on research and study. I stopped reading fiction; instead, I became interested only in pragmatic writings. Self-help books became an addiction. There was no longer any fantasy in my life. An essential part of me had died.

Since then, I have talked with any number of bereaved parents who describe a similar process taking place in themselves. That precious place they shared with their child is like a ghost town—empty and closed down.

Yet, when we are able, at the right time, there can be

a resurrection experience. First, however, we must open ourselves to the possibility.

Immortality

Our children are our tommorow. From the moment of conception—even before—we fantasize about their futures, what they will become, what they will be like, who they will marry, how many children they will have. We see ourselves in the role of grandparents. And why not? This is what we have learned to expect. This is the correct order of the universe. We count on it.

It is no wonder, then, that when our children die and the chain of order is broken, we can't comprehend it. Our future has been blunted, perhaps even stolen, buried with our dead child.

It takes an amazing amount of regenerative energy to begin to reinvest in faith, a new tomorrow, a different future. For a long time I was scared even to try.

Children Connect Us to the World

In many ways our children connect us to the outside world. They are like personal emissaries. For example, my husband was a Coast Guard aviator, so every two to three years we moved. Not long after arriving in a new place, each of the children was bringing home a new friend from the neighborhood. Then, not much later, we would have occasion to meet their parents. By then, we already had much in common with these new friends. Having children made our moves a lot easier.

What is more, children provide energy for the house-hold. Their constant enthusiasm and curiosity keep us stimulated. When we lose that energy source, it seems as if much of the world dies too. We have lost a vital source of our regenerative capacity.

PROBLEMS IN MARRIAGE

From 75 to 90 percent of all married couples have serious problems after their child dies. Just at a time when they need each other the most, partners seem to back away from each other, withdrawing their support. Unfortunately, my marriage was among those that didn't make it. The alienation between my husband and me didn't happen quickly; it was more like a slow erosion, an eating away at the side of a granite cliff until there was no solid ground left to cling to.

Of course, whether or not there will be problems in the marriage depends largely on the strength of the marriage before the death. Did the couple ever share feelings? Or did each partner keep things inside to prevent hurting the other? Were they supportive of each other or often critical? Was there ambivalence between them before the death? All these factors will either complicate or abate the grief process.

Understanding the feelings of a partner is never an easy task. After the death of a child, the job is even harder because we hardly understand ourselves. Nothing makes sense—not our feelings, not our perceptions, not even our thoughts. I'm convinced that we all go a little crazy in grief.

We all grieve differently. But even beyond that, a man's grief is different than a woman's because men and women have been socialized to fill different roles. A man is socialized to be unemotional, self-sufficient, and in control. He is the provider and protector of the family and is expected to act strong.

A woman, on the other hand, is socialized to be nurturing and empathic—the family communicator. She keeps the family circle intact. Under normal circumstances, these roles can work well because they meet the expectations of society. Yet, when partners are faced with the shattering tragedy of their child's death, the typical structure becomes difficult, if not impossible, to maintain.

In the first place, for a man to show perfect control, he must not cry. What a terrible responsibility to place on anyone, especially when his heart is breaking. Men are socialized to be more aggressive than women, so one of the first reactions for a man is anger rather than tears.

A woman's reaction is generally more passive; however, she is given full social approval to express her anguish in tears and laments. Yet she is not given approval for anger. My first reaction was to withdraw from everyone and do my crying in private. The family saw and heard me, but no one else did. I spent many hours shut in my bedroom, sobbing my heart out. This was my private grief. I wrongly reasoned that no one else could possibly hurt as much as I did because no one loved Jim as much.

We do such awful things to ourselves in grief. We are so vulnerable, so frightened, so insecure. Just when I most needed to be close to others, I shut out closeness. My protective walls went up instead, and I sequestered myself in my own private hell.

I have since learned how dysfunctional my behavior was. When we lose a child, when we lose anyone close to us, we need to share our feelings. We need to talk about the beloved person. There is no way to avoid the suffering of grief. But it is a hundred times harder if we keep it to ourselves. I urge everyone to find a support group such as The Compassionate Friends. (Chapter 14 presents a list of support groups.) Find a counselor who understands the grieving process. Find a friend who won't turn away from the pain. Remembering and sharing your grief with others is what will finally, eventually, ease the heartache and enable you to let go of your grief.

DOES THE CHILD'S AGE MAKE A DIFFERENCE?

The age of a child at the time of death doesn't seem to matter; the searing pain and inconsolable agony seem to be the same. However, complications in bereavement can occur as the result of developmental issues relevant at the time of death. What was the level of growth? Was he an infant, a preadolescent, or a mature man?

Tom and Louise's daughter was only nine months old when she died of spina bifida. The couple had nursed her through those first months with devoted care requiring twenty-four–hour vigilance. The child had become the center of their life, an important love object upon whom they doted night and day. As Louise said:

> Melinda had just started to smile back at me. To see her precious little face light up when I came into the room or watch her search my face for a smile while I rocked her to sleep was a joy I had never experienced before. Losing her is a terrible failure for us. She depended on us, and somehow we let her down.

For Tom and Louise, Melinda will always be nine months old. She died at an age when she was totally dependent on her parents. They didn't have to contend with adolescent personality conflicts but only sweet smiles or desperate physical needs. What complicated their grief was the deep shame they experienced at not being able to save their daughter. "Parents are supposed to protect their children and keep them from harm," Louise said. They both felt that they had failed Melinda and now were suffering a horrible punishment.

Roger was eighteen when he died in a car accident. He was a passenger in the back seat when the car took a curve too fast, rolled over, and broke into flames. The driver and his date were thrown out, suffered multiple injuries, but lived. Both Roger and his girlfriend were trapped in the burning car. Neither escaped.

Roger had been going through a rebellious period since he was fifteen. The number two boy in the family, he had always felt that his older brother could do everything right, but he couldn't do anything right. Roger ran with a fast crowd. His father had warned him repeatedly about chumming with the car's driver because of the driver's many speeding tickets. Roger's parents had sought help from a psychologist, but Roger was resistant. He went to only one counseling session and then refused to go again. Roger's dad said later:

> I could see something coming, but I couldn't do anything about it. I met a brick wall at every turn. I wish I had locked him up...he'd be alive today if I had. I kept hoping he'd come out of this rebellious period sooner or later—he was a good boy underneath, just really mixed up. Now it's too late.

Roger's parents not only had to deal with their terrible grief over losing their son, but also had to cope with the unfinished conflicting feelings that usually arise between parents and teenagers. Sorting out emotions of anger, sadness, guilt, and shame seemed like an endless quagmire.

The roles a child plays vary according to the child's age and the size of the family. Though issues might be different, a child's death—at whatever age—will be an insurmountable obstacle blocking the way for many years.

WHEN CHILDREN DIE SUDDENLY

It's impossible to comprehend. One day they are there—laughing, playing, teasing—and the next, they are gone. Gone without a trace of the laughter, the endless chatter. Their beds have not been slept in. There are no crumpled pajamas on the floor. The house is empty of the sound of their voices—just as empty as the hearts of the parents. The death of a child, at any age, leaves the survivors in an intense state of shock and disbelief. When the death happens suddenly, the shock can last for months. The survivors can be emotionally frozen, locked into numbness and unable to move on to the next phase of grief.

In adolescence, accidental deaths are frequent. They are often accompanied by parental ambivalence—a state of extreme emotional conflict—because the teenager is in the process of individuating, of assessing his or her own independence. The normal working through of these years is abruptly halted when death occurs. The parents may direct much anger toward the youth for being so reckless. As described, the shock reaction freezes parents' grief until they can absorb the reality of the death.

In this frozen state, the parents of the dead child may remember him or her as perfect, beautiful, and brilliant. The child may be intensely idealized. Often the parents are caught up in their fantasy for so long that they become lost in their own grief, unable to free their emotions to continue with their recovery. They remain frozen in their memory of the perfect child.

When there is a diagnosis of a terminal disease, shock at hearing about the severity of the disease is the parents' initial response. This is usually followed by a long period of reasonable denial during which they understandably push for the best treatment, the best doctors. There is a need to know as much about the condition as possible—a tremendous need to understand what is happening to their child. There is hope for a cure, a remission, or a miracle. All this gives the parents an opportunity to accept the reality of the disease. The parents begin anticipatory mourning for their child.

When the dying takes place over time, the shock of death is less intense than that in cases of sudden loss, in which there is no preparation. The pain, the agony of separation are similar, however. The parents, as primary caregivers, feel emptiness and lack of purpose when they no longer have their sick child to take care of. Their physical exhaustion often matches their emotional exhaustion.

THE STIGMA OF GRIEF

Grief carries a peculiar stigma having to do with the shame of death as punishment. Nowhere is this more evident than following the death of a child. Because a child's death is rare, when a child dies, many survivors and others feel that some cosmic force has singled the parents out for this painful catastrophic event. I remember feeling that God must have turned his back for a moment. How else could a loving God have allowed such a terrible thing to happen to my child?

I remember a neighbor who rushed into my bedroom about an hour after I got home from the hospital. She was there to comfort me, of course, but what she told me didn't help. She said that, as soon as she heard about Jim, she rushed home to gather her four children in her arms, relieved that they were safe and alive. I understand now what she felt. But, at the time, I didn't need to hear that. After she left, I went into the bathroom and threw up.

In the Tampa Bereavement study, a research project I conducted several years ago, bereaved parents told me how others would avoid them when they were out. One mother said:

I was shopping in the supermarket when I saw an acquaintance duck behind the frozen-food section just

to avoid meeting me. It really hurt when I saw that—
like I had a contagious disease.... You can't catch [grief]
for heaven's sake.

Another mother compared the period just after her
child's death to being a leper without a colony. She felt
alienated and alone. "It is just like being shunned by
the community, left out, and just at a time when I need
people to support me. It's not fair."

The age-old lament Why my child? is typical of the
meaningless torment that bereaved parents wrestle
with. If others in the community avoid grieving parents,
it is because they are frightened of the torment. People
are struck dumb when confronting a tragedy of such
magnitude. There is nothing they can do, they reason,
and their sheer helplessness leaves them feeling awk-
ward and self-conscious.

HOW LONG WILL I GRIEVE?

Trying to put a time limit on bereavement is pointless.
I'm sure most of us would like to control the grieving
time. It is hard to tolerate so much pain for very long.
We would like to say, "Okay now, I expect to grieve
for six months; then I want to move on. I am willing
to suffer, but after six months I don't want to hurt anymore."

But grief is not like that. It is a long, complex process.
So much depends on such factors as ambivalence toward
or dependence on the dead child, how many people we
have supporting us, what is the state of our health,
crises that we are faced with at the same time, how
we react to stress—a multitude of variables enter into
resolving grief. Research has indicated that the death
of a child may take years to resolve, if it can be resolved

at all. One thing is clear: Grief can't be rushed and it can't be avoided.

THE SEARCH FOR MEANING

The search for some meaning in a child's death is an ongoing rumination for survivors. It is as if we must unearth every detail surrounding the death, so we can begin to piece together this incomprehensible tragedy. When nothing makes sense, we desperately search for some small clue, some piece of evidence that will complete the puzzle.

Rarely will we find it where we are looking. Rather, meaning will be found in making a stronger commitment to life rather than looking back to death. But we won't be able to do that in the beginning.

It used to anger me when anyone would suggest that grief offered lessons that would enhance spiritual growth. That was an absolutely repulsive suggestion early on. The idea that I could grow out of such tragedy seemed inconceivable to me then.

Now I have a different perspective. I have found that really hard times test our mettle. They make us wiser and stronger by pulling us inward and giving us few alternatives but to keep going. Feeling defenseless in the face of such utter helplessness, we turn to a spiritual source of strength. Call it what you will—God, Providence, our Higher Power—we learn that our search for meaning leads us to a stronger connection with that source—that when we listen for guidance, we find it. But first we have to stop blaming, and we can't do that in early grief. Early on, we are filled with recriminations against ourselves, others, and even God. Allowing a power greater than ourselves to direct us, we finally begin to find a way through the maze of pain, loneliness, yearning, guilt, and anger.

To you who have just lost a child, I urge patience with yourself. Don't expect to have answers or reasons right away. They may never come. Be willing, instead, to go through the phases of grief, not to turn away from pain but to walk into it. As you face the long journey, it looks impossible; I strongly advise you to take one day at a time. You've heard this many times before, I'm sure, but never is it more true than when you lose a child.

Imperceptibly, growth takes place as you heal. You won't be the same person you were when your child was alive. But if you form a closer tie with your Higher Power through prayer and meditation, you will gain a strength that you never imagined possible. Having survived the worst thing that can happen, you need never be afraid of anything again. Through your grief, you develop an immunity against fear.

2

• • • • • • • • • • • • • • • •

The Five Phases of Grief

AND IT wasn't but a couple of weeks after we had gotten home from Christmas, I can't quite ... yes, it was after Christmas. And I decided that it was time to put her things away in her room because she wasn't coming home, and I couldn't stand to have that room the way she left it. So I changed the bedclothes and put something that hadn't been on the bed before, and started to box up everything. I got her books off her shelves and onto ours and then started with her toys. That's where I kind of copped out ... I just couldn't. I just went back and watched television. I wasn't really interested in what was on TV, but I couldn't be in there. I had to wait till I felt stronger.

—Bereaved mother, age 28

This chapter deals with the phases of bereavement and describes various symptoms and characteristics of each phase. Naturally, not everyone will experience all the symptoms at once, and some symptoms may overlap the phases. For example, you might carry a symptom over to the next phase or not experience a symptom at all. You might find times when you fall back to experiencing symptoms from the previous phase. You shouldn't worry about these regressions, nor fear that you are back in the deep trough of a previous phase. Ride it out, talk it over, deal with it. These small regressions are quite normal and are usually short-lived.

Knowing what the phases entail will give you some idea of where you are going in the grief process. Do not view the phases as absolutes. Use them simply as benchmarks to give you a general idea of where you are along the journey and what is yet to come.

The phases of grief outlined here are based on the Tampa Bereavement Study—a research project I undertook in 1976 in the Tampa, Florida, area—and my review of a wide variety of relevant sources. I believe the five phases are comprehensive in that they comprise the entire grieving process. Each phase offers us the opportunity for further growth. The last two phases particularly offer possibilities to push our capacities further than we had ever believed possible. We always have the option of accepting or rejecting these new areas of growth. In each of the five phases described in this chapter, I have used specific case studies to show the characteristics of that particular phase. Through these real life examples, it is possible to better understand how we progress through the phases of grief.

Facing the grieving process takes courage. But, under the circumstances, what choice is there but to be courageous? I remember people saying how strong I was in dealing with my grief. Those remarks made me angry. I had no choice but to keep on walking, and neither do you.

PHASE 1: SHOCK

Characteristics	
Disbelief	Helplessness
Confusion	State of alarm
Restlessness	Psychological distancing

Marge and Joe Walsh were sound asleep when the door-bell rang at 3:30 A.M. Joe rolled over to look at the clock. That's how he knew exactly when the police arrived. Quickly getting out of bed, he tried not to wake Marge. But she stopped him when he was trying to find his robe in the dark. "Joe, what's the matter? Who's here?"

"Not sure—I'll go check. You stay here," Joe said.

But she didn't wait. Marge had that sixth sense that plagues all mothers. She knew something was wrong.

Marge was behind Joe when he opened the door. Two police officers identified themselves and asked if they were Mr. and Mrs. Walsh. The taller officer spoke: "Mr. Walsh, there's been an accident. Your son has been badly hurt. We'd like you to come to the hospital with us." That awful pronouncement rang in their heads for months. When you hear it, you know without a shadow of a doubt that there has been a fatality.

Marge took Joe's arm. "What did he say? Is Gary hurt?" When no one answered, she looked at their stricken faces and slowly backed up. Then she began to scream. She doesn't remember any of this. Joe said later that Marge ran into the living room as if trying to escape the unwanted news. Joe told me that he tried to calm her, but when he approached her she screamed even louder. "Make them leave us alone. They're wrong. Go to some other house. There's been a mistake. It's not

Gary. He must be upstairs asleep. He's always in on time. Oh, God, no. Please don't let it be Gary." Marge collapsed on the couch, sobbing and beating at the cushions.

Joe wanted to hear what the police were saying. He wanted to help Marge, but didn't know how. He was having a hard time taking things in himself. He said later that he didn't feel anything in particular. His thoughts just tumbled over each other in incomprehensible jumbles.

Marge and Joe followed the police to the hospital. Joe had to go in and identify his son, Gary, who lay dead on the emergency-room table. Joe told me that he stopped thinking when he had to look at Gary. He was operating on instinct only. His body felt wooden, heavy. When he approached Marge in the waiting room she didn't look up, didn't move. She seemed frozen in place. Joe sat down next to her and took her hand. It was like ice. He called her name but she seemed catatonic. No response. Joe said later, "I got kind of scared then. Marge wasn't even moving, so I called the nurse over. Marge's blood pressure had dropped tremendously." They got a doctor immediately and admitted her for observation. The next day she was released. Diagnosis: acute shock.

The amount or intensity of shock we are experiencing when confronted with death is related to many things, such as our attachment to the deceased, how the death occurred, and whether it was expected or unanticipated.

When a child dies, however, the shock is amplified a hundred times. Number one, we never expect children to die. Two, because we are so deeply attached to our children, a large part of us dies with them; the grief is compounded. Three, we, as parents, are responsible for our children's well-being. When they die, we feel we have failed to care for them in a responsible way. The manner of death doesn't matter; we feel responsible for that death until we can work through the guilt.

Everyone Reacts Differently

Just as we all react differently to stress, so we all react differently to grief. Marge reacted in the beginning with shouts and screams. Later, she became frozen and couldn't function. Joe was able to respond, but he felt as if he was on "automatic pilot." Shock caused the reasoning part of his brain to close down for the moment, and he was reacting from the lower brainstem, which governs habitual action. He could do things he was used to doing, but he had a hard time reasoning out anything new. Many people function this way throughout the period of the funeral.

We Feel Confused

Shock leaves us feeling confused, forgetful. Everything that was constant before has suddenly changed. Our hearts are broken as we focus on the one who has died, and we desperately try to make some sense out of what is going on.

The Walshes managed somehow to get through the next few days. People came hourly to bring food, flowers, or small gifts or simply to support and let the Walshes know they cared.

We all experience some symptoms of shock. Marge could cry openly and often with their friends. Joe didn't shed a tear. It was up to him to take care of the funeral arrangements and, responsible person that he was, Joe carried out his duties in his usual businesslike manner. He wouldn't allow others to see that his heart was breaking. It was up to him to be strong. But he couldn't imagine why his mouth was so dry or why he found himself sighing often just to get a deep breath. He couldn't sit still. Joe didn't know that these symptoms are typical of the stress he was experiencing.

Marge said she couldn't wait to get to the funeral home to see Gary. Once there, she stood by his casket, constantly touching his hair and speaking to him in a low voice almost like a lullaby. She felt she was watching herself go through the motions during the funeral; she didn't feel as if she was there.

Marge was experiencing psychological distancing, a mechanism that protects us when we are in severe distress. It is a means we use to emotionally remove ourselves from a situation when it is too painful to face.

It is the shock reaction that creates such a long and difficult bereavement in parental grief. This phase, which usually passes after a few days to a week or two in most forms of loss, can last up to a year following the death of a child—perhaps even longer. But at some point, the shock begins to wear off, like novocaine, and we are able to gradually feel the intensity of our grief. That is when we move into the second phase of grief, the full awareness of our loss.

PHASE 2: AWARENESS OF LOSS

Characteristics	
Separation anxiety	Oversensitivity
Emotional conflicts	Anger
Prolonged stress	Guilt

Rich was only three when his parents, Irene and Ben King, learned he had leukemia. Their lives were a struggle for four years. There would be joyous times when the family was full of hope; there were other times of grief, pain, and despair. Eventually, they lost. Rich died in the hospital, his frail little body exhausted from years of treatment, his parents broken with grief and feelings of failure.

Although Irene and Ben knew Rich couldn't rally another time, when death did occur, the shock was strong. The impact is amazing. Even when we know death is inevitable, when we try to prepare ourselves for it, there is no way to anticipate how empty and awful we feel when it happens. Ben and Irene thought they were prepared. They had talked about it. They had even visualized what it might be like—the funeral, the flowers, the empty bedroom. Yet they couldn't really know the pain until their beloved Rich was gone.

Irene and Ben were fairly stoic throughout the funeral. For the six months before Rich's death, Irene had been on a leave of absence from her job as a computer programmer. Now that the funeral was over, she insisted that she return to work. Their two other children—Pam, age ten, and Robert, age twelve—were in school most of the day and, with the monumental medical bills, the family needed her income too.

Friends continued to surround and support them for several months. Neither Irene nor Ben were alone except at night, and then Irene cried herself to sleep while Ben tried to comfort her. It was just a matter of getting through one more day, one more night.

Around the sixth-month anniversary of Rich's death, Irene decided it was time to deal with his room. Up until then, things had been left as they were when Rich was alive.

As Irene opened each drawer, she came across a poignant reminder of her precious son: his teddy bear, a puzzle he had worried over, a well-worn sock with a hole in the toe. Finally, Irene could stand no more. Sobbing, she fled from the room and closed the door behind her. What Irene didn't realize was that the second phase of grief had begun. The insulation of the first phase had been torn away, and she was left feeling raw and painfully exposed.

The second phase of grief is one of intense emotional disorganization. The full awareness that your child is dead feels like an unbearable weight on your chest. You try to breathe deeply. You can't. You can only breathe shallowly. I've heard that people breathe shallowly when they don't want to feel. I remember that I didn't want to hurt, but I did—no matter how I breathed. Maybe there are certain circumstances where the pain is so deep that it is untouchable.

Phase 2 is the time when we experience the most volatile emotions of the entire bereavement process. Feelings such as anger, guilt, frustration, and shame well up inside. We feel more sensitive to what others say and react more quickly than we usually do.

When we lose a child, an attachment is broken—an attachment that was deeply integrated into our very being. It is like losing half of ourselves with no way to grow back the half that is gone. The pain of grief comes from the sudden wrenching away of that part of ourselves, and the pain is excruciating.

Separation anxiety is a major component of the second phase. Fear and anxiety are far more characteristic of this period than depression. We feel afraid. The loss of control we feel in regard to our child's death begins to apply to everything. All the things we had counted on now seem shaky and unsure. The world is no longer predictable, and we become unsure of our footing. There is no safe place.

Irene and Ben had not experienced much guilt up until phase 2, for they thought they had done everything possible for their child. However, something changed for Irene that day in Rich's room. She began to have lingering doubts about the decisions she and Ben had made regarding Rich's treatment. What if she had missed a symptom that could have changed the course of his disease had it been noticed sooner? Did they put him through too much treatment? He was such a patient little boy. He had never complained. Her heart began to ache for him in a different, more intensely painful way. As these questions continued to torment her, she had an overwhelming feeling that somehow she had failed him.

Ben, on the other hand, had no patience with guilt. He knew that they had done everything possible—to worry about past decisions now made him feel even angrier than he had been. He remembered feeling constantly helpless as Rich lay dying. He had always been assured of another treatment, another chance with Rich. Now there was none.

Since Rich's death, Ben had taken his anger out on any number of targets—the hospital billing clerk, the radiologist, God, and now Irene. He hated to see her blame herself, and the truth was that he was angry because he couldn't fix it for her. The same feeling of helplessness and powerlessness that plagued him during the latter part of Rich's life came back again in full force.

Irene and Ben began to argue with each other over senseless things. It was as if all the teamwork they had developed before Rich's death was dissolving before them. They withdrew from each other, spending evenings and weekends in separate parts of the house. Their other children, Pam and Robert, became upset, although they tried not to show it. They had never seen their parents treat each other this way. It was hard for them to believe their parents weren't arguing about them; maybe they had done something to cause the problems. Besides, Pam and Robert were dealing with their own brand of guilt— survivor guilt. In other words, they felt guilty that they had been spared and Rich had been taken. He had been such a focus of attention and love for so long that, somewhere in their awareness, they felt that he was the most important one. But he died and they didn't. And they had no one to talk with about it.

Things got worse in the family until, with the help of their minister, they were able to find a family therapist trained to deal with loss and grief. Irene and Ben learned that couples can go through what appears to be the same loss but experience different reactions at varying times. The therapist's work with the whole family helped the children move past their survivor guilt and feel that they were an important part of the family. Through expert counseling, they were drawn close together once again.

Grief uses an enormous amount of energy. For Irene and Ben, just maintaining their daily work routine sapped their strength.

Following a painful loss, our sense of security has been severely uprooted, and we feel vulnerable and unsure. This state of alarm activates the sympathetic part of the autonomic nervous system, which releases excess amounts of adrenaline. This is one reason why it is difficult to sleep or even sit still for any length of time during either the first or second phase. These phases constitute a long period of prolonged stress. Our exhausted bodies finally motivate us to move into the third phase of bereavement, a phase in which we conserve energy and partially withdraw from others. It is the only way we can recoup our used-up energy resources.

Ben moved into the third phase long before Irene did. With the help of their therapist, both were able to see what was happening. They learned not to make undue demands on each other, not to judge, but simply to allow the other to move through the grief process at his or her own pace. The therapist helped the children see that their grief was legitimate and that they had a right to feel what they needed to feel.

The shift from phase 2 to phase 3 doesn't happen overnight. One phase overlaps another. Moving into phase 3 is the body's way of saying that it is time to conserve the energy needed to deal effectively with the remaining phases of grief.

PHASE 3: CONSERVATION/WITHDRAWAL

Characteristics	
Withdrawal	Fatigue
Despair	Grief work
Weakened immune system	Hibernation

The message came to John and Sue in a roundabout way. A neighbor called at 11:10 P.M. to see if they had been watching the news. They hadn't. As a matter of fact, they had just gotten in from a Sunday-night movie and had not checked their answering machine. When the neighbor learned this she said, "Oh my God. I'm so sorry." John's heart raced as a million images hit his mind at once. Quickly he asked, "What's the matter? What's happened?" The neighbor responded with "I'll be right over" and hung up.

John rushed over to the answering machine and played the message. Then he heard the grizzly news about their oldest daughter, Mary Ann, age twenty-four, who lived and worked in Jacksonville, only a few hours from home. Betty, her roommate, sounded frantic on the answering machine as she tried to tell them what happened.

Betty had been out for the afternoon and returned around 6:30. Mary Ann had told her that she was going to read awhile and probably get to bed early that night. When Betty returned, she opened the apartment door to a scene of complete chaos. Everything was ransacked—turned upside down. She screamed for Mary Ann and ran into her friend's bedroom. She found Mary Ann on the bed, shot through the head. She realized with horror that Mary Ann was dead and quickly called the police. Because of the confusion with the police, she had not been able to call Mary Ann's parents until around 9:00.

I can only imagine the nightmare that followed for these parents as well as for Betty and the Walkers' other children—Brett, age twenty-one, John Junior, age eighteen, and Vicki, age fifteen.

Mary Ann was the firstborn and seemed special in every way. A talented musician, she was homecoming queen her senior year in college as well as valedictorian of her class. She had begun a promising career in a public relations firm. Now, none of that mattered.

The funeral was packed, TV cameras everywhere. There was no private moment for the family. After the funeral, the search for the killer continued. He wasn't found for six months. The killer was a known crack addict and alcoholic who apparently had been watching Mary Ann for weeks, waiting for a chance to catch her alone. The family was caught up in everything that went on. Their rage and indignation was visible to all.

Delay after delay postponed the trial. After the proceeding finally occurred, it was declared a mistrial because of some technicality. In the end, a second trial sentenced the man to die—he had already been charged in four other rape cases. It took two years after Mary Ann had been murdered for her killer to be sentenced.

Anger was the largest part of their emotional trauma. We can only imagine their fear and anxiety before the killer was caught. Family members felt guilt and shame as they tormented themselves for somehow not preventing the tragedy. The Walkers stayed on this emotional plateau until the trial was over. Then they finally allowed themselves to notice that they were physically decimated.

When John and Sue finally began to let down the defenses that had kept them going, they hit bottom with a thud. The third phase—conservation/withdrawal—had begun as their bodies and minds told them they needed to rest.

The problem with the third phase is not recognizing that the need to rest is a positive step rather than a negative one. The physical reaction seems so like depression. However, phase 3 is a natural time of withdrawing from others, needing more time alone, and sleeping a lot. By the time most bereaved persons reach this phase, they expect things to be better, for grief to abate. The disappointment comes when they realize that the opposite seems to be happening. The energy of the first two phases has disappeared, and they need to give in to the fatigue they are experiencing. After the near exhaustion of the preceding phases, the need is to pull back and conserve what little strength is left until rest can restore former energy. This doesn't happen overnight. The third phase can go on for months. It can be a time of dark despair because physical and emotional defenses are seriously diminished.

Somehow, after the trial, the Walkers thought they would feel relief that everything was over. This was not the case. They were glad to be out of the spotlight, but they didn't anticipate the crushing despair that hit them. There was nothing more to be done, and a sense of sheer futility settled over them. Would anything ever matter again, they wondered?

As so often happens after a prolonged period of stress, Sue contracted a virus so severe that she ended up in the hospital for a week. When the first two phases of grief have been protracted and intense, as they typically are in the death of a child, the immune system is weakened. The body has used up vast quantities of emotional and physical energy and is now without proper defenses. This is the reason that it is so important to sleep and rest rather than push beyond already weakened limits.

The next few months were a time of family closeness for the Walkers. They talked and cried together, sharing their memories of Mary Ann. Going over and over the details that come to mind is an integral part of grief work. The ruminating and unfocused sifting of memories is central to the third phase of grief. As we talk over the events surrounding the death as well as our remembrances of the one we have lost, the death becomes more real. We begin to accept the fact that the child is gone forever.

For the Walker family, the horror and violence surrounding Mary Ann's death left them with a double threat. Not only did they have to deal with the ghastly events of her death, but they had to face their realization that, at any time, the order of the universe could be reversed. The remaining children felt vulnerable and afraid that something violent could also happen to their parents or to them. Sue and John worried constantly that something could happen to another one of their children. The Walkers' was a very complicated grief to survive but one that was balanced with a most unusual, courageous family.

Through the closeness of this family, each member was able to gain strength as time went on. This is not to say that the family never argued. Far from it. There were many times that opinions clashed, feelings were hurt, or accusations welled up. But rather than denying or ignoring the tensions, they tried to help each other process the negative emotions.

It took longer for Sue and John to work through the third phase than it did for the other family members. The children had their own lives, and their friends helped them move out into the world once again. They recognized that they were feeling stronger and wanted to go on with their lives.

It has been three years since Mary Ann's death. Sue does not try to rush the process, but she has patience and faith that, in time, she will be able to resume her life fully. Things will never be the same for any member of the Walker family. They don't know at this point in their grief just how much changing still needs to be done within themselves.

But a turning point has been reached.

PHASE 4: HEALING

Characteristics	
Taking control	Forgiving and forgetting
Giving up old roles	Searching for meaning
Forming a new identity	Closing the wound

Tommy was at summer camp, the first one he'd ever attended, and he was having a wonderful time. Everyone in his family thought he'd be homesick, but he wasn't at all. He entered wholeheartedly into the spirit of the camp, growing more enthusiastic by the day. One of his favorite activities was to swing on a big rope that had a large knot on the end. A kid could swing out over the banks of the river and, if he wasn't too scared, drop into the water ten to twelve feet below. Use of the swing was well supervised by the camp counselors.

But one day when Tommy was swinging, the rope broke and dropped him onto some large boulders. Tommy landed on his head.

For two days he stayed in a coma, hovering between life and death. Late in the afternoon of the third day, he died. His parents, completely in shock, were with him when he took his last breath.

Tommy had a sister five years old, only two years younger than he was. But to his father, Tommy was special. He was his father's namesake, a carbon copy of Tom Senior. Everyone knew how special Tommy was to his dad. Alice, Tom's wife, loved to see them together, but she wondered if he bragged about Tommy too much.

When Tommy died, it was as if Tom died too. The rage came first. Tom wanted to sue the camp, especially the squad leader who was supposed to watch over the boys, but no one could prove negligence.

When the lawsuit didn't work, Tom railed against God. He quit going to church and gave up all outside activities. He withdrew into himself and even shut Alice out. When she would try to discuss anything, even things not associated with Tommy, he became angry and exploded at her. It was as if he waited for anything that would allow the anger to come out.

This emotional state continued for 2½ years until one Monday, as he was returning from work, he was involved in a very bad three-way accident. Tom's pelvis was crushed, both legs were broken, and his collarbone was broken in two places. He was in the hospital for months, just getting to the place where rehab could begin working with him. He didn't seem to want to try to help himself. He told Alice that, if Tommy couldn't walk again, then neither should he. It was almost as if Tom considered his situation just punishment.

Tom was a heartbroken, beaten man who had lost his future when Tommy died. All the plans he'd made for the two of them—now everything was gone. Because he couldn't let his grief show to others, he had to deal with his pain aggressively in angry outbursts. There was no way he would let people see him cry.

One day about five months after his accident, Tom was in his wheelchair, sitting outside his hospital room. They wheeled a cart by him with a small child on it; she was covered with bandages. A victim of a severe auto accident, both her parents had been killed. She was their only child. Tom talked with me later about her.

At first I tried to ignore her. I didn't want to think about another hurt child. But, I don't know, something drew me to her, and I asked the nurse every day how she was doing. Not well, it seemed. One day, about a month later, the nurse asked me if I'd like to help by reading to her. She wasn't responding well, and they felt that someone's voice would help her become more in touch with them. At first I said no. But a couple of days later I thought, What if it were Tommy? and I told them okay.

So, I wheeled down to her room and the nurse handed me a book. I looked at the title: *The Velveteen Rabbit*. The story was about a stuffed toy that always wanted to be real.

I glanced over at the small figure under the blankets from time to time. So small to have so much happen. I kept on reading though—and I came back every day and read a little more.

Tom was beginning to think about Tommy more and more. Tommy wasn't much bigger than this little girl when he lay dying in the hospital. He thought about how small he had been lying, so still under the blankets. Such a little form.

One day the little girl, whose name was Sarah, asked him to move closer while he read. In the middle of the story, she asked him to hold her hand. This was more than he could take. Tom broke then. Tears flooded his eyes, and he barely got back to his room before he really began to sob. He cried as he had never cried before.

He got no sleep that night as thoughts of Tommy exploded on his mind. The next day, filled with a new determination, he wheeled himself down to the chaplain's office. He was in the mood—finally—to talk, and the chaplain listened to his whole store empathetically. The more he talked, the more Tom wanted to. He came back the next day, and the next.

The chaplain helped him see how he had been holding on to Tommy with his anger and guilt until he had turned the anger toward himself in a serious, potentially destructive way. He had just about driven Alice away and abandoned his daughter, Carrie.

Healing comes slowly, imperceptibly. Most often we aren't aware of any real change. Perhaps a small bit of new energy quickens within us from time to time. We might feel an awakening interest in something. Maybe renewal comes because our bodies are more rested and the previous phase has exorcised so much sadness. For whatever reason, at some point, whether it be three years or fifteen, we will arrive at a place of healing.

Still, there is much to be done in bereavement during phase 3. As we step out of our passive hibernations, we begin to take more control over our lives. But there are roles that need to be surrendered; a new identity is required for each of us. We are not the same people we were before, but who are we? This phase is one of searching for meaning in the loss, forgiving as well as forgetting the awful circumstances that surrounded the death. Maybe hardest of all, this is the time to close the family circle—to join hands with the ones who are here and focus on the living rather than on the dead.

Tom continued to read to the little girl who gradually began to rally. In the weeks ahead, they became good friends. When she had to go to rehab, he went with her. He even began to work out in rehab himself to give her stronger motivation. Tom admired her courage, for she continued despite the pain of the exercises.

Tom had to go through much forgiving. He had to forgive the camp, and he even had to forgive Tommy for allowing the accident to happen. He had to forgive himself for not being able to protect his son from dying. He also had to say goodbye to Tommy and let him go. That was the hardest task of all because it was part of himself that he was letting go. But until he did that, he wasn't ready to live again.

During this time, and with the help of Sarah, he opened his heart to his own little girl, Carrie, once again. He realized that he had shut down emotionally as a way of protecting himself from more hurt. If he shut everyone out, there would be no one else to lose, he had reasoned.

By the time Tom left the hospital, he was walking with a cane—slowly and falteringly—but under his own steam. He kept coming back to the hospital to visit his little friend until, one day, he was able to see her walk out of the hospital too. Her grandparents had come from Canada to take her home with them. She would grow up in her mother's childhood home.

Tom had been able to heal the terrible gaping wound that had stayed open since Tommy died. He had to release the role he had built as father to a son and begin to build new roles in that place. Living without Tommy meant restructuring the person he had been to give birth to the new person he was becoming.

This shift in identity doesn't happen without resistance. The loss of a child requires more restructuring of identity than any other loss. Our identification with our children is so strong that it takes years to actively let go of that connection.

It is the letting go, however, that finally allows a shift in identity. We gradually start to take an interest in other things, new hobbies, our other children, our marriage (which normally deteriorates because spouses heal at different rates). Tom, his wife, and his daughter were able to go into family therapy. They each had a chance to share their feelings, forgive, and rebuild themselves into a stronger family unit.

The turning point for Tom was facilitated by a small, helpless child in the hospital. Through Sarah, he was able to touch his own vulnerable center that he had kept protected and closed off for so long. Through this process, he was able to use the strength and courage that was available within himself while letting go of his own need to control the outcome.

Tom had spent all his time trying to find a reason for his son's death. He now turned his attention toward searching for meaning in his son's life. It was now possible to try to determine what his own life meant. Tom had turned the corner of phase 4 and was ready to move to phase 5, that of renewal.

PHASE 5: RENEWAL

Characteristics	
Developing new self-awareness	Focusing on inner needs
Accepting responsibility	Reaching out
Learning to live without	Finding substitutes

Meg was thirteen when she disappeared. She left the house around 3:30 in the afternoon to walk to her 4:00 piano lesson. She always left a little early so that she could go by the mall near her teacher's house and see the beautiful doll collection at the Doll Boutique. She was never allowed to go to the mall without a time limit because her parents worried about the kids that hung out there.

Dinner was ready as usual at 6:00 P.M., but Meg wasn't home yet. Judy, Meg's mother, called the piano teacher. Meg had never arrived. Alarmed, Judy called Meg's best friend. She hadn't seen her. Now Judy became frantic. When Meg's father, Jim, got home, he called the police. They both got in their car and went searching. The search went on all night, the next day, and the next. No leads even. It seemed that Meg had completely disappeared.

For the next few days they waited for a ransom note. As the search went on, the prospects of finding her grew dimmer. The police reasoned that she was either out of the state by now or dead. Meg's parents refused to give up and kept the search going longer than the police wanted to.

In five weeks' time, everyone except Meg's folks had given up. The police had other cases to take care of. Meg's parents hired a private detective who stayed on the case for three months. He turned up five false leads that took them nowhere.

Judy and Jim had gotten little sleep since Meg's disappearance. They were reluctant to sleep for fear some news might come in. This constant worry, heartache, and intense stress began to work on them. They wouldn't allow themselves to believe she was dead, but there was no proof that she was alive.

Every time a small clue would crop up, they would have a burst of hope. But hope always led back to despair. Judy and Jim, like other parents who have literally lost a child, found that getting through this kind of loss is endlessly excruciating. There are no rituals, no clearly defined markers to show you where you are in the grief process. You can't even grieve properly because, as yet, you're not even sure a death has taken place.

Eventually, Judy and Jim had to dismiss the private investigator. They just didn't have the money to pay him.

For Jim and Judy, the despair of the third phase kept slipping back into rage or guilt. It took several years to arrive at a place where they could really give up the idea of ever finding Meg. While this recognition was a time of hopelessness and despair, it was also a place for them to let go and begin to turn to the future.

The phase of renewal for Jim and Judy couldn't even begin until they were fully able to give Meg up into God's care. They needed to affirm their trust that she was being taken care of. They had done all that they could. Now they needed to let go.

Grief is like a death and resurrection experience. As the old roles and identities are released, new wellsprings of life trickle up within us. We are not the same people as before, but within us we have the potential to develop a new strength that will spread over all our relationships and activities. We become more tolerant and have deeper compassion to share with others. The phase of renewal provides the opportunity to develop new self-awareness while, at the same time, we develop a healthy emotional independence. In essence, we must take responsibility for our own happiness if we are to find it.

Jim, growing up as the oldest son in a family of four, had always assumed the position of the responsible one. Trying to succeed had been very important to him, and he had done well in his career. After his loss, however, everything about his job lost its flavor. With Meg's disappearance, he realized how much time work took from the things he really wanted to do, such as gardening, fishing, or just relaxing. He loved to be outdoors working with his plants. Jim had always promised himself he would build a greenhouse, but he had never had enough time. His first priority had always been to provide for his family. What he wanted for himself stayed in the background. Jim dealt with his healing phase by reducing his office work slightly. He worked in his garden and spent more time with Judy. He needed her more emotionally than he needed her physically now.

Judy came to see how she had always wanted her mother to be proud of her. Ever since Judy's father had left home when she was eight, she had taken over the role of making her mother happy. Her interest in returning to school for graduate work was twofold: Judy wanted to make her mother happy and she wanted to make Meg proud of her. She worked very hard to accomplish both goals.

Judy kept on going to school after Meg disappeared, to keep her mind off things. After she received her Ph.D., she taught English part-time at a local community college, but her interest in teaching waned.

The turning point came for this couple almost five years after Meg disappeared when they took a vacation at a small inn in the Georgia mountains, an inn they had visited before. One reason Jim loved the place so much was that the owners grew most of the vegetables they served. They were always appreciative of Jim's gardening help and suggestions for a better harvest.

But when they arrived this time, they found the owners upset: Their main helper had quit the day before. Jim offered to help in any way he could. The outcome was that the two couples became good friends during the week, and they even talked about Judy and Jim becoming partners in the inn.

Jim went home happier and more rested than he could remember, Judy had become involved in the financial end of the operation by helping in the office, something she'd always wanted to try. They talked endlessly about the offer. How could it be done? What would they be throwing away? What if they failed? How could they sacrifice all the years of study and experience at their jobs? And there was perhaps the most burning question: What would their parents say?

What began to happen for Judy and Jim was that they were in the process of giving up their old roles as parents of a daughter, as caregivers for their parents, as conventional husband and wife. Instead, they gradually began to come to a new self-awareness that gave them the confidence to move on with their lives—not the same old lives that had been lived for others, but new lives that focused on inner needs. A sense of adventure they had never known began to take over. They could not stop thinking of the possibilities. Eventually, they resigned their jobs, took their savings, sold their home, and went into partnership with the inn owners. It turned out to be a most successful venture, not only in terms of money but, most important, in happiness and satisfaction.

Their values had shifted in the five years since Meg

had disappeared. Now they learned that, if they were to be happy, they each had to accept the responsibility of making themselves happy. And though they could share their feelings, support one another, and develop a closeness they had never dreamed possible, they could never accept responsibility for making the other one happy. They were beginning to have emotional independence, which allowed them to focus on the positive aspects of their new freedom. There were times in the beginning when they felt guilty that their behavior seemed selfish, but they helped each other to remove the conflict by supporting their individual positions. As an extra benefit, for the first time in years, they enjoyed passionate lovemaking.

Certainly, there were anniversaries when they were both caught in a poignant memory of Meg. Her birthdays and Christmases were hard for many years. But Jim and Judy learned to live with these painful reminders by being there for each other, empathizing and listening. Meg was never forgotten, of course, but the memories, except for a few sad times, were now focused on the special gifts she had brought to them for those wonderful thirteen years.

Jim and Judy had moved through the process of grief and had each answered the inner callings of their own child within. For the first time they had listened to what they truly wanted to do with their lives; each had followed the inner child to a new peace.

Predicting how long it will take anyone to complete the process of bereavement is hard. I was extremely resistant to the process. It took me nearly twelve years. But then, I had no knowledge whatsoever of how to deal with grief, how to help myself. Most important, I did not know that, not only is it okay to share grief with others, it is imperative. If I had approached friends sooner, they would have been there for me. But I couldn't tell them what I needed, because I didn't know myself.

When our child dies, it hurts more than anything we can imagine. In the beginning of grief, we are destitute because we can't know that the pain will end. Certainly, there is no assurance that it will ever end.

But it does. We have to learn much along the way before we can move through the process. We must learn patience, the value of change, the beauty of simplicity, the importance of laughter, the life-sustaining strength of relationships, and the joy of spontaneity and adventure. We have to remind ourselves that, deep down, each of us is a child that must be nurtured.

Probably grief's most important lesson is faith—faith that, even in the blackest moments of despair, a clearing will appear somewhere up ahead. There will be better times—they do come. I can promise you that they will.

3

• • • • • • • • • • • • •

Dealing with Guilt and Anger

YOU SEE, *we never went down that street. It was just an unspoken rule. The accident happened on that corner, and we always wanted to avoid it . . . just too painful. But it was really strange one day. I got the strangest urge. I was driving a big truck. This guy was riding shotgun with me, and he didn't know anything about how I felt. But anyhow, I was going down a street near there on my way to pay my car insurance, and I got to looking down that street and I got to thinking: Nothing in hell's going to keep me from going right past it. And I couldn't figure out to hell with who or to hell with what, but I was determined I was going to do it. And I did. . . . And when I passed that corner, I laid on the horn—a big old air horn. I forgot what he said, something like "What's wrong? There's nobody there. What did you do that for?" And I said, "Just for the hell of it."*

This defiance is kind of interesting because I had this feeling as though something beyond my control, beyond the world, had really done a dirty, lousy deal. And I had no control over it. And when I would feel like shaking my fist, it wasn't to anything in particular, but maybe just to the total frustration of this thing happening and not being able to fight back decently with it. It's such an uncontrollable situation that you're in.

—Bereaved father, age 35

Guilt and anger are among the most common and powerful reactions that a parent has to the death of his or her child. The two emotions are really two sides of the same coin: Guilt is anger turned inward.

This chapter will discuss the types of guilt and anger, under what circumstances each is likely to appear, and what you can do to heal from these emotions.

GUILT

After Jim died, I was filled with gut-wrenching guilt. I didn't know why. It didn't make a lot of sense. I hadn't caused my son's death nor had I contributed to it in any way. But somehow, I not only felt enormous guilt, but it seemed also that I felt ashamed—ashamed that I hadn't protected my child enough. Other parents had healthy, living children. What terrible sin had I committed to be punished this way? What had I done to cause this terrible tragedy? It wasn't until many years later that I learned how much guilt and shame we take on ourselves as bereaved parents.

One of the reasons for this is that we are brought up in a society that believes and expects parents to be totally responsible for their children's care. If something happens to them, we, as parents, feel that we are at fault. We feel we should have been taking better care to prevent such harm. The terrible sense of failure when we don't live up to society's expectations leaves us feeling guilty and ashamed. It is as if we have done something irreversibly wrong; caused the harm; or, at least, did not prevent its happening.

Mary and George both worked at IBM. As a matter of fact, that's how they met. They often worked on projects together, becoming good friends in the process. George said later that he knew he had strong feelings for Mary during this time but, because she was married, he never spoke of them to her. When Mary became pregnant, she shared her unhappiness with George, telling him how she had planned to leave her husband months before but was always waiting for the right time. Now this.

Mary learned that she could share many thoughts with George and found a receptive empathizer. Before too long she realized she was in love with this very considerate, caring person. She left her husband and, on her own, found an apartment.

Through it all, George was there for Mary. It was George who went through Lamaze with her. It was George who was there when her baby daughter, Mitzi, was born. It was George who cared for them both and stayed nights to take turns giving the baby her 2:00 A.M. bottle.

George and Mary were married when Mitzi was six months old. There was never a problem associated with his stepfather role. George was as devoted as any natural parent. Mitzi's own father had disappeared to parts unknown before Mitzi was born; George was the only father she would ever know.

On a December afternoon 4½ years later, Mitzi was playing with her friends in the yard. The children were out of school for Christmas vacation, and Mary had taken some time off to be with her. Mary was intermittently watching Mitzi and doing the wash in the laundry room just off the garage. The neighbors had a swimming pool which, of course, Mitzi had been warned about time and again. They had not yet covered the pool for the winter.

Mary, to this day, doesn't know how the accident happened. It was all so fast, she doesn't remember the time sequence. One of the children raced excitedly into the laundry room, screaming for her to come outside quickly: Mitzi had fallen into the deep end of the pool.

By the time Mary got Mitzi out of the pool and started CPR, Mitzi was lifeless. There was no discernible breath. A neighbor rushed to call 911. Through it all, Mary kept the mouth-to-mouth resuscitation going. Later, in her journal, she wrote what she was saying to herself as she tried to save her daughter's life:

> Mitzi, please don't die. You can't die. God, she's cold, so cold. Mitzi, breathe, please breathe. She's gone, I know it. No, it can't be—she can't be dead. Help me, God, help me! You can't be dead. Oh God, this is real. It can't be!

The rescue team arrived quickly, or so a neighbor told her later, but to Mary, it was an eternity. No matter what they did, nothing helped. Mitzi was pronounced dead at the hospital. A physician offhandedly told Mary, "By the time you brought her in, it was too late to help." He probably didn't realize it, but he shifted the blame off himself and onto Mary. Those terrible words never left her mind.

Mary couldn't deal with her failure. She couldn't face the reality of the event, so she vacillated between denial and wishful yearning that nothing had ever happened. There is nothing unusual about that response; it is the norm rather than the exception in early parental grief. But, for Mary, the denial escalated. Because the guilt was overwhelming, she had to invent a way to help her survive. To protect herself, Mary moved into total denial. She denied that she had ever really loved Mitzi. She said she didn't really care that Mitzi was gone. She was ready to get on with her life free and unhampered by children. This was a bizarre way to deal with guilt, but it was the only way Mary knew. She simply removed herself from the situation.

George told me that at first he didn't even notice Mary's reaction, his own grief had been so deep and painful. As it continued, however, he urged her to see a counselor, offering to go with her. Reluctantly, she agreed, but she explained immediately to the counselor that the couple was there to help George deal with his grief. She was fine.

Fortunately, the counselor was not only able to help Mary break through her denial and deal with the guilt but was also able to help the couple process their grief together. They told me later that they became very close during this time and openly discussed their feelings. They let each other know when they were hurting. This opened a deeper level of intimacy in their relationship, helping them cope with the vulnerable emotions that were still so raw.

The two of them began attending meetings of The Compassionate Friends, a support group for grieving parents. At the meetings they could share their experience and receive support and understanding from others. Mitzi is ever present in their hearts, and they feel certain that one day they will be able to take out all the photographs George made of her and keep them out. Until then, they will keep up their practice of taking them out only on special anniversary occasions.

Mary's denial was caused by guilt brought on by her perception that she had failed to live up to others' expectations of her as a mother. She should never have allowed Mitzi near the water. She should have gotten Mitzi out of the water sooner and to the hospital before it was too late (the doctor in charge had made that clear). All these "shoulds" added up to guilt overload, a burden Mary could not carry and continue to function. So she blocked all her feelings for Mitzi. By denying her love, she could escape the guilt.

Guilt About Helplessness

Our helplessness, our inability to save our children, generates guilt. One father said to me: "I stood by Janey's hospital bed, praying—begging, really—for my little girl to be healed. I offered everything I owned if God would just make her well again. No matter what

I did, it didn't work. I had to wait there helplessly as she grew worse each day."

This father had always been able to fix things, to make them better. But now, he was totally helpless. Because of this, he suffered terrible pangs of guilt for his seeming inadequacy.

Survival Guilt

This form of guilt comes from the firm expectation that our children will naturally survive us. Thus the continuation of the species is ensured. When this pattern is broken, when a parent survives a child, the parent feels tremendous guilt. Each parent questions the meaning of his or her life. A parent asks Why should I be allowed to live when my child can't? Who will carry on the family name? How can I ever enjoy anything again, when my child has been robbed of a future?

After Jim died, I remember feeling that I didn't have a right to laugh again. But hardest of all, I felt that my life wasn't worth anything compared to the budding potential of my son. I couldn't understand why I had been spared. It didn't make sense.

Trying to avoid the pain, I plunged into a frenzy of activity, trying hard to find a reason to be alive. Unfortunately, I wore myself out. Then I had another source of guilt to deal with: my own "inadequate" stamina, which I felt was a flaw.

Guilt About Ambivalent Feelings

The word *ambivalence* refers to conflicting feelings toward anyone or anything. No person feels pure love or perfect acceptance all the time. Many times we feel angry, out of control, or resentful toward our children.

This is perfectly natural. However, after a child has died, our memories of these emotions swell up to gigantic proportions, and we admonish ourselves for ever feeling ambivalent. The self-torture that follows is often relentless.

Helen, a young mother whose month-old baby died of sudden infant death syndrome (SIDS), remembered times when she had ambivalent feelings about whether she should have had a child at all. These emotions were particularly prevalent the first few weeks after the child was born.

I thought I would never get enough sleep. I was exhausted all the time, and Suzie demanded so much attention. She always did. I was overwhelmed with so much responsibility.

Then, after she was gone, I couldn't believe I had felt that way. I was too ashamed to talk with anyone about it. I really hated myself.

I'd give anything to be up at night with her now.

Helen suffered from these ambivalent thoughts and the guilt they caused for a long time. It was after she had finally shared these feelings at a group meeting of SIDS parents that she began to see that they weren't unusual or bad. Little by little, she was able to release herself from uncalled-for guilt.

John suffered in the same way when his teenage son was killed in a skateboard accident. He blamed himself over and over for being too hard on the boy, saying: "If I had spent more time being with him instead of yelling at him, he might be alive today." Endless torment.

In parental grief we lose sight of the naturalness of our conflicting feelings for our children. Only with constant reality checks—by constantly comparing our fallible perceptions of reality against the way life really is—can we finally release ourselves from this tenacious source of guilt. And we can't do it alone. We need the help of others who both understand and can be more objective than we are.

To rid ourselves of guilt, we must accept the fact that we are human. To be human means that we can dislike our children sometimes as well as love them. No relationship is perfect love. We are not perfect saints. We cannot free ourselves from feeling guilty about past ambivalence until we accept the fact that we are not saints.

Guilt About Perceived Misdeeds

Joanne had had an abortion six years before Karen was born. When Karen died of leukemia at age four, Joanne felt the death was her punishment for having the abortion.

Joe stopped going to church when he was seventeen. He had found it to be a bother and couldn't believe in a lot of the principles his folks lived by. But ten years later, when he lost his son in a drowning accident, he blamed himself for betraying God, feeling he was being punished now for leaving the church. His parents cemented this feeling by reaffirming these sentiments several times during the funeral services.

Oftentimes, guilt is intensified when bereaved parents have used alcohol excessively. When they lose a child, they feel victimized, unable to separate their alcoholism from their child's death, seeing the death as punishment for their disease.

Another perceived misdeed that parents often punish themselves for is busyness. Parents who have failed to spend quality time with their kids may feel that they lost their children as a punishment. Sometimes this guilt is instrumental in helping the parents develop better schedules and create more leisure time with their remaining children. More often than not, however, the habit of staying busy becomes even more intense.

Guilt About Our Reactions

As we struggle to find a way through the pain caused by the loss of a child, we may not act in ways we think society expects us to act. Our perceived failure to act the "right" way may make us feel guilty.

Before Jim died, a couple we knew had lost a child. The parents held two wakes, one in the town where they lived and a second one in their hometown in Illinois. Since we had had little experience with death, we were appalled by the parents' openness at such a private time. We vowed then that, if anything ever happened to either of us (we couldn't even admit to the possibility of losing a child), we would have only a closed casket and no wake. We felt anything more would be too painful for the survivors. How little we knew about the need to grieve, the need to be a part of the funeral rituals, and the need to commemorate the life that had been lived and was now gone.

At Jim's funeral, we had a closed casket. I never saw him after the accident. It feels terrible to think about it even now, and it did then, too. But I was too stunned to comprehend much when the accident happened. All we could remember was the way we had felt when our friends' child died. Later, I felt ashamed that I had not seen my son. I carried this feeling deep within me, however, and never mentioned it to a soul until two years later. At a meeting of bereaved mothers, I felt safe enough to share this confidence. One woman turned to me with a surprised look touched with a degree of horror. She said, "You mean you never saw your child again?!" I turned red and stammered some response. I did not speak about the matter again for many years. I'm still sad that I didn't see Jim. It was a mistake. I would like to have said goodbye in person, and I believe the reality of his death would have been clearer. The worst, however, was the guilt and shame I carried for not living up to what had been expected of me.

I remember a young mother who talked with me at a conference where I spoke. She too had been holding in feelings of guilt. Hers had to do with overreacting (as she called it) at the funeral. She was ashamed that she couldn't have been more stoic. Her in-laws had been extremely critical because she had cried so openly and kissed her small child as she lay in the casket. I tried to reassure her that her response was most appropriate. Whatever she did was fine. It was her own expression that counted, not what others thought she should do. Anything we do to get through our shattering tragedies is okay. Just surviving is all we can manage. There are no right or wrong ways, just each person's way. And that is the best way because it comes from the heart.

Codependent Guilt

Codependent behavior originates in early childhood. If one or both parents were emotionally withdrawn, the small child perceives their behavior as emotional abandonment. The feelings of the child live on within the adult, causing a fear of further pain and abandonment. The adult buries the longings of the inner child in shame and guilt—for protection against future abandonment— he or she is fearful of commitment in all relationships.

A large number of us have been brought up in dysfunctional families and have developed codependent personalities. As such, we often become people-pleasers, controllers, caregivers, or extremely self-reliant individuals. We develop these roles out of guilt—guilt that we aren't adequate, that we don't measure up to our parents' desires. We feel that we owe everything to our parents or that we need to continue to repay them. In a sense, we go through life punishing ourselves for never having been able to make our parents totally happy. We stay in a state of perpetual guilt.

When we are codependent to start with and then lose a child, guilt is intensified. If we are people-pleasers, we bend over backward to do everything others want us to do. If we are controllers, we cannot accept help from others because we're too busy deciding what everyone else should feel and do. If we are caregivers, we become enmeshed in taking care of everyone else's grief. We are too busy comforting others to care for ourselves. If we are compulsively self-reliant, we stay too busy working for others, taking responsibility for them; we do not allow ourselves to grieve. These behaviors do not relieve guilt; they augment it. What's more, we continue to believe that we are grossly inadequate.

For further information about codependent behavior, please check the reference section toward the back of this book.

Letting Go of Guilt

Keep telling yourself that you did the best you could under the circumstances. There is no perfect way to be a parent. It takes courage to open up your secret places by admitting that you can be less than perfect. Opening up your secret places brings discomfort at first. In the long run, however, you will feel more at ease. And best of all, you will be letting go of crippling guilt.

When you carry guilt, you are responding to the inner child, who is afraid of abandonment. What is disquieting about this situation is that it is you yourself who is abandoning the inner child. When you lack the courage to face your guilt, you punish yourself more than you realize. You fear what others will think or do, so you keep your guilty thoughts to yourself.

Guilt seems to develop naturally in grief. This section has examined the most common types of guilt from which grieving parents suffer. Many more forms exist.

No matter the type of guilt, however, if it is chronic, it is destructive. The best way to exorcise guilt is to share guilty feelings with supportive, caring people. If you hold guilt inside, it festers and becomes increasingly destructive. To expiate guilt, expose it to the health-giving properties of light and love.

ANGER

As this chapter has discussed, guilt and anger are closely related. Which comes first often depends on personality and gender. Women are discouraged from showing anger. Rather, they are trained to be "nice." Because females have held the roles of nurturers, peacemakers, and soothers, women who openly express anger are thought of as "bossy," "controlling," or "bitchy."

The taboos against a woman's anger are so powerful that, most of the time, she doesn't even know when she is angry. As a result, she learns to fear anger. She fears it because it brings such disapproval from others and because she is afraid it will make matters worse.

For a mother who has lost a child, the prohibition against anger blocks the most natural as well as the healthiest emotion she can show. Holding anger in often results in serious emotional as well as physical problems primarily because she turns the anger inward, toward herself.

Men, on the other hand, are raised to be more aggressive. Young boys see their fathers expressing anger and learn that it is all right to do the same thing. Of course, boys are not allowed to express anger inappropriately with adults (we still have our pecking order). But with peers anger is considered appropriate. Boys who don't act out some anger during sports or games may be classified as wimps. So anger become a natural response when men face frustration or helplessness.

Ben and his son David were partners in a law firm that Ben's father had started. The partnership had worked well from the beginning. They each respected the other. David had great admiration for his father. Ben, from the days of David's early childhood, rarely let his son down. Ben's wife, Edith, was a kind, loving woman who drew the family together like a warm hearth. Life was comfortable and fairly predictable.

Who could predict, however, the crash of the commuter plane that carried David home from a business meeting in Milwaukee? Ben and Edith learned about the crash even before passengers were identified; they saw the report on TV news. The pronouncement "There were no survivors" took their breath. They sat stunned for a moment. Ben jumped to his feet to call the airport. The line was busy. He brushed by Edith without a word, jumped in his car, and headed for the airport. Arriving, he tried to get out on the airstrip, where he could see the blackened plane—smoke still rising from it. He was stopped. Ben suddenly saw someone he knew, a supervisor at the airport. He rushed over to him and spoke the first words since he had seen the news report. "David's on that plane. Help me get out there." He didn't recognize his own voice. It sounded shrill, an octave above his usual pitch.

David was one of the first to be pulled out. He had been dragged from the plane and was lying under a blanket, badly burned, barely recognizable.

Ben's story came out later. He remembers going a little crazy and yelling at everyone in sight. He said he tried to pick David up to carry him to an ambulance, but others held him back. He swore at anyone who came near. Ben, usually a quiet and rational man, lost all perspective. Anger was the only emotion available then, and it served him well at the moment. Though he didn't get what he wanted, anger allowed him to release the surging, powerful shock that had filled his being. Nothing he could do, however, could save his son.

Ben's was a long and difficult bereavement. His anger and frustration took him from one vendetta to another. He tried to sue the airline. Then he tried to sue the airport, then the town itself for allowing the airport to be so near the dangerous cliff that created difficult air currents for incoming planes. He got no satisfaction.

Ben used his anger until he was completely worn out by it. By that time, Ben's rage had taken him where he needed to go, by acting as a safety valve. In time, he moved into the third phase of grief, a quieter place that allowed him to rest and deal with his feelings in a more appropriate, subdued way.

Displaced Anger

The bereaved often displace anger onto people or things that had nothing to do with the death. Even in a case where no one is to blame—in a case of disease or accident where others were not even involved—many grieving people need to find something or someone to rail against. The hospital staff, the doctor, the ambulance driver, or the funeral home are frequent targets. God takes His share of anger too.

Sometimes, the recipient of the anger recognizes the need for the bereaved to ventilate and takes the tirade with a grain of salt. The bereaved person is probably better off risking others' wrath and releasing anger than trying to stomach the raw emotions. Holding the anger in can cause serious physical problems.

Another way to displace anger is toward the dead child. Part of our feelings of helplessness stem from the fact that we often have no one to blame. A bereaved mother shared with me her enormous anger at her child's recklessness in driving too fast. "He didn't value his life and that makes me really mad. After what I went through to get him here, too." Parents of a suicide victim are usually, and quite naturally, angry at the deceased child. "How could he do this when he had his life still in front of him, with everything to live for?" "How could he abandon us after we have tried to be good parents? How could he punish us like this?" Suicide is an agonizing grief that carries with it high intensities of both anger and guilt.

Anger About Being Deprived

The death of a child means loss on many levels: a part of oneself; the future; a love object, both in giving and receiving; and oftentimes, the main reason for living. Losing all these valuable parts of life at one time often causes a feeling of deprivation that seems impossible to deal with. The result is helpless rage.

A large part of our loss depends a great deal on the unconscious sense of ownership we feel for our children. The phrase "This is *my* daughter" is more often felt literally rather than figuratively.

A bereaved mother told me, "When we lost our child, we lost someone who belonged to us. He was taken away even though we fought to keep him. Now we feel as if we have lost everything of value. We were cheated, and there is nothing we can do about it." Helpless rage. I remember that feeling so well. I was angry at God, at myself, my husband, at the other boys who were still alive. Why was I deprived when other families were still intact? God, why did you take my child? I thought of my son as mine. I had carried and delivered him. I had cared for him through colic, chicken pox, a broken arm, falls, and stitches. In my unconscious, I believed he was mine.

But he wasn't mine. He was, instead, loaned to me for a while to learn from, to love, and to grow by. We don't own anything, really. Not our homes, our cars, our parents, our mates. We have been allowed to share them for a while, but at some point we must give back everything we have borrowed—sometimes even our children.

It took me awhile to assimilate these thoughts, and maybe a little longer to fully believe them. But once I did, I was free of the helpless rage that had plagued me after Jim died.

Anger burns itself out eventually. We can't physically maintain a rage without becoming totally exhausted by it. We must listen to our bodies. They will tell us when it's time to rest. Anger is a safety valve for overwhelming frustration, deprivation, and helplessness. However, if carried on too long, anger loses its benefits and can eventually destroy us. We need to listen to our bodies to make sure this doesn't happen.

One word of caution. We can sometimes feel guilty from having demonstrated anger toward others. When this happens, we are simply reversing our anger and turning it toward ourselves. Once we experience the anger, we must learn to let it go. Maybe simply explaining to others that you needed to ventilate your anger at the time you did will stop the guilt. If you were vindictive toward another, follow the tenth step of the Alcoholics Anonymous program: When we are wrong, promptly admit it. This keeps guilt from taking over.

Anger About Being Out of Control

Most of us rely on maintaining some form of control in our lives. Whether we control ourselves, others, or the environment, control is the means we use to keep our world in order. When we lose a child, we feel as if there is no stability anywhere. Worse, we lose all faith in people, things, and places. We feel as infants must, with no control over anything. We have only anger.

Grief is a regressive phenomenon. The many losses

incurred in one death catapult us back into early childhood. Our helplessness at feeling so out of control causes enormous anger.

Letting Go of Anger

As we are able to survive grief and start a new life, we begin to gain some control again. We feel some confidence returning. Yet, the most important lesson we can learn from grief is how to let go of control and live with more spontaneity. We live more easily when we give up the notion that we can control others or even our environment.

When you let go and allow a Higher Power to take control, you can be amazed at how quickly anger is dispelled. Your inner child is relieved of major external responsibilities. You are free to take care of yourself.

There is no way to avoid guilt or anger when a child dies. Whether the child was never born or middle-aged, our feelings are intense as we are hurtled back into emotions of childhood.

Yet we don't have to suffer long years of pain because of guilt or intense anger. If we try to understand our fears related to shame and abandonment, we can find the root of our pain and begin to heal ourselves.

We will need others' help in dealing with guilt and anger. But one word of caution. Make sure the people you choose to support you are people you can trust: other bereaved parents, a counselor who understands grief, a loving and patient friend. In your vulnerable state of grief, you need trustworthy friends so you can learn to trust again.

While you are grieving, the world is an unsafe place. Choosing trustworthy supporters takes time and practice; don't delay. Delay only strengthens negative emotions. Healing will come. Courage will come as well, little by little, as you take each small step forward.

4

• • • • • • • • • • • • • •

Unresolved Grief

MY BABIES were lying there on the road, both of them. I went screaming to them, but someone grabbed me and said I should wait for the ambulance. They wouldn't let me go to them no matter how I struggled. I didn't even know that I was hurt too . . . that the truck that had hit us had destroyed my car. I only knew that my children were lying hurt in the road. Later, I learned that they were both dead.

—Bereaved mother, age 32

She left my office that day, a fragile-looking woman, bent
as though she were carrying the weight of all humanity
on her shoulders. And she was. Three months earlier her
house had burned down, taking her husband and two
children with it. Her husband, in an effort to save her,
had pushed her from the second-story window as she
screamed for help to the neighbors. Her only injury was
a broken arm—and a broken heart. Her children, her
mate, her house, her possessions—even family pictures—
all gone. She was completely alone in the world. For some
reason that only God knew, she had been left alive to
survive, seemingly devoid of purpose or hope.

I've written in earlier chapters about the reasons for
the severe reactions in child loss: the strong bond between parents and child, the sense of responsibility that
parents have for caring for their child, the guilt and
shame survivors inevitably must live with, the parents'
belief that they have failed, their lost future, and the
parents' identification with the child. When parents lose
a child, they lose a large part of themselves. Resolving
all these issues takes an enormous amount of time and
energy—and pain. Resolving the loss of a child is a
hard, slow process—harder and slower than any other
imaginable.

Given all this, one wonders how any bereaved parent
can resolve the child's death at all. Some never do, and
those parents confine themselves to an interminable hell.

In my research involving grieving parents, I have defined four types of grief that have the potential for being
unresolved: inhibited, or suppressed, grief; distorted/con-
flicted grief; unsupported grief; and chronic grief.

INHIBITED GRIEF

Resolution requires you to learn to live without. You
must give up not only your beloved child but also the

many facets of your relationship with your child: your role as mother or father, your love object, and a source of love. These are only a few of the many attachments. And so, before you can resolve grief, you must let go of emotional involvements with your dead child. It is extremely difficult to give up emotional attachments to one who meant so much. For some it is impossible.

Jane was a single parent who was raising three children with little financial help from their father. She had divorced him when her youngest son, Michael, was almost three. John, the middle child, was six and Melissa, the oldest, was ten. At the time of the separation and divorce, Jane had asked for very little. Just being away from her husband was a relief. He was a practicing alcoholic who was physically abusive to her and the children when he was drinking.

Jane had worked before the divorce but, afterward, had to take overtime hours to earn enough to pay the bills. Melissa was her right arm through all this, helping after school with housework and getting dinner ready. When Jane worked late, she would pick up Michael from the babysitter's, drive him home, and go back to the office after they had eaten together.

As the children grew, Jane relied more and more on Melissa's help. By the time Melissa was fifteen, she was taking full care of the boys after school and doing the housework too. Jane and Melissa were like sisters in the way they cared for the boys. They were extremely close and shared more than most mothers and daughters. Jane wondered how she would have ever made it without her and acknowledged that Melissa was a gift from God.

Graduation from high school was a high point for Melissa. She was valedictorian, and her address was one of the best in the history of the school, everyone said. Jane almost burst with pride.

The graduation dance was special that year because the students had hired a live five-piece band. Melissa's boyfriend looked like he could love Melissa forever, Jane told her neighbor after the couple left for the dance. The very thought of Melissa marrying and leaving brought a quick lump to Jane's throat.

Jane's phone rang at 2:00 in the morning. Could she please come to the hospital—there had been an accident. Melissa had been seriously hurt. "Some mistake? Oh no, Ma'am, I'm afraid not. The young man, her date, gave us your phone number. We have her purse, too. Your daughter is Melissa Harris, isn't she?"

Jane was at the hospital for the next five days. Melissa lost ground each day and died on the sixth day after the accident. Jane's life seemed to go with Melissa's.

How could Jane live without Melissa? Their lives had been so intertwined. Melissa was Jane's best friend. She had been a coparent for the boys, in many ways a surrogate spouse for Jane. But most of all she had been a wonderful, loving daughter—a part of her. There was no replacement for Melissa, who had a role of such importance. Jane depended on Melissa. Now she had to learn to live without her or use illusions to block reality.

Jane chose illusions. Jane pretended Melissa was only away at school. The boys humored her at first, but when the fantasies continued, they became angry. Finally, they moved out. Michael was then almost seventeen and Roger was twenty.

Seven years have passed since Melissa's death. I wish I could report that the boys came through unscathed, but that didn't happen. They both used drugs and alcohol, had several scrapes with the law, and earned poor job records. Neither has finished high school.

Jane had a nervous breakdown and entered a psychiatric facility for treatment. Her illusions of a live Melissa caused the entire family a tremendous amount of irreparable damage.

Resolution of grief calls for us to acknowledge the reality of the death. We don't want to do this. We will take every opportunity to find some other answer. But once the reality sinks in, we must face the fact. The beloved child is dead. This is why it is so important to view the body. Confronted with this truth, most of us accept the proof of reality. In fact, in many cases we must have this proof to begin our grief work. Until a loss has been acknowledged, there is no definite proof of loss. This compounds the suffering of families of missing children or servicemen who are missing in action. These families hold out hope forever, thus putting their own lives on hold.

Resolution also calls for us to experience the pain. There is no way around it. If there were, I'm sure everyone would opt out. It is a horrible gut-wrenching pain of such severity that it can only be termed indescribable. It doubles us up, and our chests ache with a searing pain. We gasp for air as if the wind has been knocked out of us. Why would anyone invite this pain?

Embracing the pain, going toward it and through it, is the only way to come out the other side. The pain is finally what heals us. It acts to cauterize the emotional wound and allow the bruised and mangled soul to recover.

Fortunately, the body demands a respite from pain on occasion and gives us a time-out. When our attention is led to other things for a short period, or when we find ourselves enjoying something temporarily, then it is important to allow the distraction to happen. These time-outs help recharge our energy, which we badly need for the work of grief.

DISTORTED/CONFLICTED GRIEF

When Jim died, I was a typical example of someone who avoided the pain of separation. But rather than avoiding it by creating delusions as Jane did, I became a whirlwind of activity. Oh, I hurt of course. I cried a lot at times when others couldn't hear or see me. Driving to and from class was a good time for me to cry.

Yet I wanted to be in control. I controlled by taking charge. Having four children had given me ample opportunity to practice, and I imagined that it was obviously my "take charge" ability that had allowed me to accomplish so much in life. Staying busy seemed to me the best way to maintain psychological as well as physical health. In the past, if I became depressed, I would simply step up my activities. It had always worked before. The only problem was that sometimes I became exhausted, and I would need to cut out all activities for a short period. It never occurred to me to learn to balance my life, nor did it occur to me that I was trying to avoid anything.

So it seemed a natural response for me to stay very busy after Jim's death. Besides taking four courses at college, I taught a young adults' Sunday school class on Sunday evenings. I continued singing in the church choir and sang a solo only two months after Jim died. I was still in shock, and I was doing what I had always done with my pain: I numbed it.

But perhaps the most damaging thing I did to myself was to stop talking about Jim. At school I could be anonymous. At home, we stopped saying Jim's name. It was as if he had disappeared from our lives. How strange a reaction it seems to me now. He was on our minds constantly, yet we thought the pain would go away if we didn't acknowledge our grief or verbalize his existence.

It was ten years before I began telling my story at meetings of The Compassionate Friends support group— ten years before I began to resolve my grief. In the sharing of grief I found the help I so desperately needed. Only until then could I truly acknowledge the loss and begin to search for meaning in Jim's life and mine.

During the inhibited ten years after Jim died, I had stopped talking to God as well. I thought my Higher

Power had turned away from me and left me to fend for myself.

After that, as I told my story over and over, my pain was diminished. In talking with others, I realized I was talking with God more. I finally saw that He had not deserted me; it was the other way around. I had stayed so busy, I had distracted myself from everything of any meaning. When I began realizing this truth, I began slowing down and facing the pain I had sought so diligently to avoid.

UNSUPPORTED GRIEF

Social support is one of the primary aids in adequately resolving a major loss. When support is plentifully provided, when we can share our loss with our community, it appears that bereavement can be eased and its length shortened. However, when we must suffer our loss alone, when the community shuns our grief or we shun our community, then we feel much the same alienation and shame as do tribal members after a "bone pointing." This is an ancient practice of punishing an offender by total isolation, by acting as if that person no longer exists. The person who no longer has a connection with his community often chooses to go away and die rather than live an "invisible" life. Likewise, if our community does not support our grief, part of us "goes away" to die. Without this part we can never resurrect ourselves through grief resolution. The loss of a child is most certainly a death of the parent.

Unsupported Grievers

Among those groups who find themselves shunned by the community after a loss are parents of murdered children, parents of children who commit suicide, parents of missing children, and parents of those who are missing in action (MIA) in the armed services. These are the unspeakable deaths or losses that no one wants to acknowledge.

Another group of unsupported grievers include single parents and families new to the community. The support network for these two groups may not be broad enough to provide lasting help. And a major requisite for social support is that it continue over time. People who show up to help in the beginning and thereafter keep their distance can be useful (for a little support is better than none), but they do not constitute a support system. Adequate support requires that we have people there to listen, nurture, and offer their nonjudgmental help whenever they can. Supporting a grieving parent requires perseverance because there is no time schedule for grief.

Another group of parents who receive no support for their grief are those who have suffered loss through miscarriage or abortion, or mothers who have given their babies up for adoption. These are the silent grievers who must carry their pain alone.

I will focus on all of these groups in more detail in later chapters, but it seems important to include them here under the category of unsupported grievers. It is my continued wish that no one go unsupported through an ordeal as traumatic as the loss of a child. When grief goes unacknowledged, we as bereaved parents are cast into chronic pain, unable to find meaning in life or death and unable to move on with a new life.

Parents of Murdered Children. Living with the memories of what the child must have suffered before death—the fear, the pain, the pleading for mercy—this is what parents of murdered children are left with.

The public aspect of this death encompasses your life.

Your child is no longer your child; the child becomes an aspect of the hunt for the killer, the trial, and the long aftermath of fears and anxieties. The hunt can go on for years, as can the trial, as can the appeal. Parents of murdered children keep grief open until something is settled. When the murderer is never apprehended, grief is like a chronic cancer that eats away at the core of being.

Because murder is such a horrible, tragic death, the family is often left alone. Friends find the death unapproachable.

Parents of Suicides. Suicide is the death that every parent feels he or she could have stopped. There is an absolute and total sense of failure. There are also strong feelings of personal rejection and of unworthiness and shame because you have not only let your child down, but you have also let society down. Had I been a better parent, the survivor thinks, a more caring parent, a more responsible parent, my child would be living today.

With so much self-denigration, parents of children who commit suicide often shut themselves off from social support, even though they are yearning to be close to others. There is sometimes a feeling that they are "contagious" and that to be around others would only spread this bad luck to someone else. Shame runs deep. This is the paradox that parents of suicides live with: wishing somehow to heal the pain but, at the same time, not feeling that they even deserve exoneration. Yet, resolution depends strongly on sharing with others. Guilt and shame are only eradicated by exposing them.

Parents of Missing Children. According to the National Center for Missing and Exploited Children, approximately 15 million children are missing each year. These children come from every walk of life. A large number are never found. One day the child is there; the next, the child is gone.

Rarely is the child perceived as missing initially. Rather, there is the search in various places where he or she surely must be. Only slowly dawns the realization that the child is gone.

In these cases, grief is put on hold for months—even years—before the parents can face the fact that they will probably never see their child again. The normal grief pattern is delayed and disrupted so that support for these parents diminishes dramatically. When they are ready to grieve, there are few people left to be there with them. The support had been directed toward helping them find their child; few people have the capacity to turn their perspective around to help them let go of the child, a much more painful kind of support.

Parents of MIAs. Parents of servicemen missing in action follow the same pattern as those whose child is missing, except they don't live with the same self-denigration or feelings that they haven't been responsible parents. Nevertheless, they suffer feelings of helplessness, loss of control, and anger.

One difference that can be noted in the families of MIAs is the lack of support for parents. Generally, what support there is goes to the wives and children. However, a parent's grief may be more severe and chronic because the wives and children of missing servicemen can eventually build a new life.

This is not to say that wives and children of MIAs don't suffer incredible pain, loneliness, and anguish. I'm just suggesting that the parents of MIAs are not given the social support they need for the long process of their grief.

Single Parents. I remember calling on a young mother of a teenage boy who had drowned in a boating accident at a nearby lake. As she said:

I have lots of single friends who try to understand what I'm feeling or at least guess they do, but they just don't. They tell me to keep myself busy—go out more, as if that will help. I'd just rather keep by myself, then I don't have to pretend how I feel.

This woman's ex-husband was now living in Alaska with a brand-new family. He was definitely unavailable. Her family lived in another state and was not able to visit very often. She felt completely alone.

As the numbers of single parents grow, perhaps there will be greater recognition of the isolation and extreme loneliness felt by parents who must bear their grief alone. Parents Without Partners is an excellent group that can offer help in such situations.

Parents Who Are New in a Community. Families who lose a child when they are new in an area can be as unsupported as single parents because they, most often, have not had the opportunity to develop a committed support group. To cry with people or allow them to see us in a rage requires trust, and trust takes time to build.

Thank goodness for support groups like The Compassionate Friends that simply accept us as we are—as suffering bereaved parents.

Parents Who Suffer a Miscarriage. People often think that because a baby is never born, there is nothing to grieve. A woman who has miscarried is often told "You can always have more" or "Maybe it's just as well. It probably wouldn't have been healthy." These comments are meant to comfort. Instead, they tend to anger the mother who had already fantasized about what her baby would be like, even look like. Very quickly the loss is forgotten by everyone except the grieving couple. They must deal with it in the best way they can.

Those Who Undergo Abortions. Like miscarriage, induced abortion is not considered to be a source of grief. Unlike miscarriage, abortion is usually kept secret and carries with it a sense of guilt and shame. Society gives those who go through an induced abortion no liberty to acknowledge grief or loss. Needless to say, society at large rarely helps a woman deal with her loss when she has chosen abortion. Even when the abortion is performed for medical reasons, people sympathize with the mother by telling her how lucky she is not to be having an unhealthy baby—they do not comfort her in her loss.

Mothers Who Relinquish Children to Adoption. Often the loss of the birth mother is overshadowed by the joy and excitement of the adopted mother. The birth mother's grief can be all but forgotten, and she must act as if nothing has happened. However, a great deal has happened, and the problems she must face in coming to terms with her feelings are many. The birth mother has carried the baby to term and knows this child on a deeper level than anyone else. The process of realizing the loss is obstructed because the baby actually exists. She may not be able to talk about the baby with anyone or express the helplessness she might feel. Often the event has been kept secret, which does not allow for ventilation of emotions like anger or guilt. To add to this, she seldom has support from family. Society offers no sympathy, and she is alone.

The Responsibility for Support

Unsupported grief sentences bereaved parents to untold suffering. Having a caring and nurturing individual near when we are in grief lessens the grief. Recognizing this, each of us has the responsibility to be aware of situations of unsupported grief. When we can form a nurturing cushion around one grieving person, we ease an enormous pain. Beyond that, we pave the way for that grieving person to move toward the resolution of bereavement and allow him or her to carry on the support to someone else who needs it. It is worth the effort.

CHRONIC GRIEF

Marie had always been a fearful mother. She had always worried about Jody's well-being. When he had chicken pox, she sat up with him all night. Her husband, Richard, thought her behavior was somewhat overdone, but he went along with her just to keep peace.

He did put his foot down, however, when he thought it was time for Jody to have a bike. All Jody's other friends had bikes; besides, biking would be a fun thing for them to do together. Jody had been a mamma's boy too long, he said.

Marie was furious for a week when Richard came home from work on Jody's tenth birthday with a brand-new bike in his pickup. Jody was ecstatic. He wanted to take it out right away, so Richard got his bike out and they went around the neighborhood, showing off the wonderful blue and silver ten-speed. Jody couldn't have been happier or more proud. Marie finally conceded that the gift was okay, but she was still very apprehensive.

Then one day about six months later, Jody decided to ride home from school by taking a new route. Suddenly, at the end of a steep incline, the road turned to soft gravel. Jody was thrown over the handlebars, hit some rocks that had been moved to the side of the road, then fell down a steep embankment. He wasn't found until later that day, when some road workers on their way home saw his bike. When they found Jody, he was dead. A severe concussion and a broken neck had killed him.

Marie had been worried sick since 3:30, when Jody usually came home. At 5:00 she had called the police. Nothing. She began calling his friends then. No one had seen him. By the time Richard got home at 6:30, she was nearly crazy. Not much later the police arrived to ask them to come to the hospital. There, Marie and Richard learned the tragic news. Richard saw Jody and even held him in his arms for a moment. He told me later that he didn't even feel like himself doing it; he felt as if he were only watching himself go through the motions. It was, perhaps, the only way he could do what needed to be done.

Marie was inconsolable. She locked herself in her room and refused to see anyone. Richard could hear her crying constantly. She talked to Jody, called his name, and kept his pictures around her. By this time, Marie had moved into the guest bedroom and came out only to get some food. She would not talk to Richard or accept any food he offered. She said she hated him. She told him it was his fault Jody was dead and that she would never forgive him.

Richard, in his usual passive state, figured this would pass. Marie's mother came to stay for two weeks, but like Richard she made no headway with Marie. This was Marie's grief alone, and she wasn't letting anyone in.

Marie refused to let Richard change anything in Jody's bedroom. She kept the door closed and shades drawn. Then, about six months after Jody's death, Marie began going to the cemetery every day. Richard said he thought that her getting out was a good sign at first, but as her daily visits continued month after month, he became more concerned.

Three years later, nothing much had changed. Marie would not go for help, still blamed Richard for Jody's death, and still maintained Jody's room as it had been. It was as if she was waiting for Jody to come home and wanted everything to be the same.

The last I heard from Richard was to tell me that he had pretty well given up on changing anything. Marie was the same, and he was exhausted. He was considering a divorce.

Marie was choosing to remain in deep pain. If she held onto her pain, she thought, she could hold on to Jody. She had never accepted that Jody was dead. Marie's case is an example of chronic grief. Marie could not accept the final separation from Jody. Separation was worse than the pain she lived with.

In looking at Marie's fearful personality before the death, we can conclude that she had little faith in the world to begin with. She had faith only in the incidents she could control. When faced with Jody's death, something that she couldn't control, she could manage only by clinging to a few parts of her own environment.

By placing the blame on Richard and keeping her anger alive, she could control him, too. She interpreted his passive behavior as guilt. When he accepted the guilt she attributed to him, she could maintain a reason for Jody's death: He died because of Richard. Her interpretation justified her fearfulness. She had convinced herself that she could never trust anyone but herself.

Marie found purpose in life by keeping Jody alive now that he was not physically present. She took care of the cemetery plot, planting flowers in summer, keeping the bird feeder full in the winter. She even put out a bird-bath and insisted that the grounds keeper put water in it, although she was there to do it every day. At home she kept Jody's toys dusted and arranged. She even washed and ironed Jody's clothes when she changed the spreads from season to season. All this behavior directed toward Jody distracted her from herself. Marie's way of coping was a self-perpetuating system designed to guard against reality ever creeping in.

We must let go of denial if we are to resolve our grief. We must let go of emotional involvements with the dead child. Letting go is a process that is extremely difficult for most of us. When we are in grief, we feel more insecure and out of control than at any other time in our lives. Feeling out of control causes us to be afraid.

Letting go of control and being out of control are two entirely different things, however. Being out of control implies a total loss of control over everything—ourselves, our environment, others. It is something that happens against our wills. On the other hand, letting go of control is an act of faith. It means that we trust our Higher Power. We believe that whatever is happening, whether it is the intense pain of grief or guilt from the past, it will be lifted from us eventually. Patience is the hallmark of the ability to let go.

When we let go of denial, we are changing a hard grief into a soft grief. Hard grief keeps us on guard, our backs stiff, our anger and resentment in full force. It also keeps us stuck in the past. Because hard grief is based on fear and denial, it does not bring about resolution. Instead, it builds walls and obstructs forgiveness and compassion.

Soft grief is the acceptance of pain. It is the acknowledgment of separation and the need to rearrange our lives to fit the present reality. Soft grief is intensely painful, but—once it is over—healing takes place. Soft grief provides the climate for love and forgiveness. Soft grief never takes away our feelings, but it does allow us to use them to encourage and move us to the healing resolution we, as bereaved parents, all seek.

5

. . . .

How Families Grieve

LIKE MY family's Protestant, her family's Catholic. And we had a friend who is a minister, a personal friend of my family and a personal friend of ours. And he is a Baptist minister. Anyway, he came all the way from Tennessee to be with us and help us through the funeral. . . . He was a great comfort to us. But to please her family, because they were insistent, we were going to have a Catholic Mass. . . . The priest came and said that he was really unprepared . . . which irked me. We got through the service somehow. I was really mad at her family for being so stubborn. The funeral really had no meaning to us whatsoever.

—Bereaved father, age 45

How can a family function when one of the links is missing? The truth is, it can't. The abyss is so wide and we become so alienated that members need help in building bridges to one another again. The family structure crumbles after a death. Members must gain a new and different balance. So much depends on readjusting ourselves to the empty place not only in our hearts, but in the family system.

The family is held together by the roles we play. For example, one child may play the role of peacemaker. Another child may take responsibility and "manage" the other siblings. Each role is important to the family's stability and balance. As you can imagine, when one of the family members dies, his or her role is left open. The entire family is affected and falls into temporary chaos. The family struggles for some sort of equilibrium. The smaller the family, the greater the number of roles each member must fill. Without the large extended family of the past—in which nearby aunts, uncles, and cousins abounded—today's children are more important in the family's linkage than ever.

As one bereaved father explained:

> I had no idea Tommy had become such a focus for our interest, our love, our everything. I knew we paid a lot of attention to him. He was learning so much every day. But still, he was so young. He had only been with us a year and a half. Such a short time—I can't believe how much I miss him—what I'd give to have him back. Just to hold him again. I don't see how things can ever be the same again.

This man probably doesn't realize it yet, but things will *never* be the same again. That little chunk of space that Tommy occupied will always be there. No matter how we try to replace, replenish, or rearrange it, we are still caught in the ever-present poignant reality that my child "was," therefore my child "is"—somewhere.

NEW ROLES THROUGH COMMUNICATION

The only way to develop new roles within the family is through communication. The communication styles of families differ greatly. For closed families, where communication is perceived as a danger, grieving is more difficult than in open families, where survivors express their feelings.

Closed Families

Members of a closed family have learned to keep secrets. For example, if the parent is alcoholic, the family is taught to keep this truth private. Family members don't bring friends home and rarely plan a gathering that includes outsiders. If we have this orientation to family life to begin with, we handle all crises in the same private way. This situation can result in any dysfunctional family, alcoholic or sober. These families attempt to keep up a good front for outsiders while hiding the truth about anything unpleasant. This same attitude applies to a death in the family. If a child dies, the silence and denial escalate. A family that keeps secrets usually views the death of a child as a form of punishment. This type of family focuses on never allowing others to see the pain—of remaining "strong" and stoic. After the death the family tries to secure as much control as possible, and this usually means carefully controlling feelings and the amount of talk. Members fear trusting anyone.

This attitude keeps the closed family from receiving social support which, as mentioned, is of extreme importance to grief resolution. Friends and neighbors don't intrude when they realize they are not wanted. Family members are left with only themselves—no help at all since they don't talk to each other. With this lack of openness, family members drown in individual sorrow, never realizing that to save themselves from chronic grief, they must reach for the lifesaver of support. Bereavement is a time when friends are necessary.

Gene was a practicing alcoholic. His buddies were all good old boys who congregated at various houses on weekends to watch football or whatever sport was in season. Their weekends began Friday night and wrapped up Sunday evening after they had consumed vast quantities of beer. Monday morning was always a hell for them as they trudged back to work.

Even so, it was a greater hell for Jan, Gene's wife, whose dream of the wonderful marriage that could have been was slipping away, silently and slowly. Having been brought up in a different kind of household, she dealt with her embarrassment by using a heavy coat of denial most of the time. Her marriage had taught her much about the value of keeping quiet, of retreating into her private life. She taught her children the same survival patterns.

As a result, they were all poorly equipped to grieve the death of the oldest son, Kenneth. At age twenty-one, Kenneth totaled his car after a college fraternity party. He was drunk when he hit the tree. A shudder of guilt at feeling responsible was very quickly covered by a heavy layer of denial. As long as Gene could bury his feelings, keep other people out, he felt a level of control.

Unfortunately, our defenses get more brittle with time and eventually crumble under the weight of stored emotional baggage. I would like to say that Gene got into treatment, but he didn't. Jan, on the other hand, left the marriage with her two teenage daughters after six months. Al-Anon was a salvation for Jan and the girls as they learned the lifesaving quality of support from other family members as well as new friends. It wasn't until then that Jan could even begin the long uphill climb of resolving her grief for her lost son.

It takes emotional courage to resolve grief. And we can't do it alone. A bereaved mother wrote:

> Before we went to Ohio, Phoebe was telling us how she never hears from anyone in the family except us and how she can't understand it. I guess that is one of the biggest things that bereaved parents have to deal with: the family. I don't know how it's been with anyone else's family, but I identify with Phoebe. It is so confusing to bereaved parents to know that your family loved the child who died . . . and then chose not to express that love ever again. They don't realize that it may be easier for them, but it sure is harder for us. We have enough to cope with without losing our family, too. It's like this in more homes than it is the other way. They don't know what to say so, therefore, they say nothing—or perhaps they choose to say things about how God wanted another flower for his garden, and he chose our child. Well, I don't know about you, but statements like that made it worse for me. I believe with all my heart that when we are feeling hurt because of the neglect our families show us, we had better get on the phone and talk with another bereaved parent. There is too much at stake. [Family members who don't understand] are strong enough to stand behind their ignorance, but we are too weak so we have to stand behind each other.

I cannot emphasize enough the need for communication. One of the most important things we can learn in life to prepare us for the griefs to come is to drop the walls of privacy and rid ouselves of the fears that keep us silent prisoners in our own tiny worlds. When we realize that it is our childhood fear of abandonment and rejection that keeps us walled up, we have the opportunity to let go of our tight control in not only our lives, but others'. Actually, this is not merely an opportunity, but rather an obligation we owe ourselves. We then give up the fight against our fears and let God direct our actions. Our families will grow tremendously as we share our journey with them. Who knows, even the most closed member may gain a toehold in letting go of some of his or her private thoughts. Sometimes this miracle happens to families during a profound loss: They learn how to open up to one another. When families can do this, their path to resolution of their grief is made not only smoother, but shorter.

Open Families

God bless the open families. They are the ones used to sharing their thoughts and feelings. They are the ones who openly admit to their pain and their negative thoughts, the ones who don't build walls or shut others out. They are the positive teachers for us all.

When a family system is open, the members' thoughts and feelings can be related without fears of rejection or abandonment. There is no fear of being made fun of. They can be honest about their grief, sharing openly and often. There is no fear either that the memory of the beloved child will die, because they have faced and come to terms with the reality of the death—they are not afraid to face their pain. They have each other to lean on.

A family I met during my research in the Tampa area was able to do this. When one of the ten-year-old twins in this family of four children contracted bone cancer, there was not too much time left to learn this lesson of openness. They had been a fairly closed family, financially well-to-do, seemingly without worries. The mother and father were socially prominent, avid golfers who spent most weekends on the golf course. The children were taxied to and from endless lessons and practices by a sitter. The family came together at mealtime, which was a hurried affair.

When Dennis was diagnosed with cancer, he was hospitalized for several weeks. Family members curtailed their activities immediately. There was a major awakening between the parents during this hospital time as they began to see how distant family members had become in their busy lives. Feeling some urgency, they talked with their minister, who suggested a family therapist whom they should all see, including Dennis. In the beginning each was reluctant to risk hurting anyone and scared to expose his or her own vulnerability. It was Dennis who led them to be more fearless about their thoughts and feelings as he began to ask them questions about his disease, pleading for them to be honest with him.

As Dennis's disease progressed, the family members grew stronger in their mutual bond. The paradox was that, as Dennis grew weaker physically, he appeared to grow stronger in his family's love. Death was not the feared enemy any longer—silence was.

This family was able to continue in its strength after Dennis died, sharing the pain and loss, helping each other—always remembering, they said, the lessons Dennis had taught them.

WE ALL GRIEVE DIFFERENTLY

One thing that is so hard to remember is that each family member grieves differently. This is primarily due to the fact that each person's relationship to the lost member is so different. An older sister has quite a different relationship than a baby brother. Each parent experiences a different loss which, in turn, generates dissimilar griefs. Instead of being able to share the loss completely, spouses are not usually synchronized in their grief response. One may be up emotionally while the other is down, or one may pass through one phase faster than the other. A spouse wrongly concludes that he or she can't depend on the partner for help in grieving. Both partners just try to take care of themselves.

Yet, grief is unquestionably a family affair. We are all affected by the loss—sometimes, in what might be seen as a domino effect. The grief of one member triggers the grief of another, and so on. Whole households are often caught in acute grief as tensions escalate. Many times when this happens, tempers are short and irritations flourish. People say things they don't mean, and family feuds begin that can last for years.

Sometimes it isn't the family that offers the biggest comfort, but another bereaved parent. Other parents who have lost a child know what it's like. They can listen patiently as the grieving person describes the pain. They won't try to fix it because they already know they can't.

One couple, who are bereaved parents themselves, wrote persuasively of the need for open communication:

> I believe that it is up to us as bereaved parents to let society know how much we need them and count on them for their support. I believe we can do this in a positive way so they too can grow. It is about time that everyone stop hiding behind the statement that they don't know what to say or do. We have to tell them lovingly that death is part of life. We don't know when or who it will happen to next, but we had better know how to help so that we can be a loving and compassionate society. We are the experts, the professionals, because we have been there.

The Grief of Fathers

Jack wasn't macho, but he certainly was a man's man in many ways. He was an athlete in high school and college. He even considered going into pro football for a while but decided on a steadier line of work after he met Julie during his senior year. In a magic time for them both, they fell in love and made plans for a future together. Everything went smoothly for them for many good years.

When the children began arriving, Jack was a responsible and loving dad. He took his turns with the 2:00 A.M. bottle, bathed the children when he got home from the office if he didn't have a golf or basketball game, and offered to help Julie whenever he could. However, it was up to Julie to manage the household. His jobs were taking care of the family financially and fixing things when they broke. Theirs was a traditional marriage.

They had three children, when Jack Junior's accident happened. To celebrate his fourteenth birthday, he had been allowed to go on a ski weekend with his church group. He was a competent skier and natural athlete, so he had no hesitation about skiing the most difficult runs. That day, however, he caught an edge on a narrow turn, fell, and plummeted into a tree headfirst. Jack Junior never came out of the coma.

Julie was overcome. Shock took over for the first few hours, but it wore off before it should have. Raw pain sliced at her heart like a steel blade. She vacillated between panic attacks, during which she couldn't breathe, and hysterics, when the pain in her chest was so intense she felt she was dying—and didn't really care if she did.

Jack reacted in an entirely different way. He immediately stepped into the role of taking care of things. He made all the arrangements at the funeral home. He explained what had happened to the other two children and comforted them. He watched over Julie like a hawk. He was the one to call family members and friends to tell them the tragic news. Through it all, Jack remained strong, composed, and emotionally controlled. For several weeks Jack managed in the same controlled manner, his own grief placed in a holding pattern while he took care of everyone else.

The first signs of Jack's breakdown were short outbursts of irritation and anger, both on the job and at home. He seemed to be running from himself all the time. Often now, he would stop at a bar on his way home from work, something he had never done before.

Julie hardly noticed, because she was so caught up in her own grief. However, his peers at work saw a changed man. They were all too often the brunt of his angry attacks. Finally, his boss arranged a quiet dinner for just the two of them. He carefully probed Jack's feelings. At first Jack resisted, maintaining he was just tired. His concerned boss kept on prodding, however. Abruptly, Jack said, "Let's get out of here" and was on his feet in a second. By the time his boss had paid the check and got outside, he found Jack leaning against the side of the car, sobbing relentlessly—no longer able to hold back the avalanche of tears and pain. Jack was in a therapist's office the next day. He didn't need hospitalization; he was able to take an extended leave of absence while he finally came to terms with his own feelings.

Jack talked with me later and shared some of his thoughts and feelings after Jack Junior's death.

I was devastated, but I couldn't let down. My gosh, Julie had fallen apart. One of us had to take care of things—help the children. But I couldn't seem to make sense out of anything anymore, everything was out of control. I was used to taking care of things, now I felt a failure because I couldn't fix it. I couldn't keep my family from all the pain they were suffering. My beautiful son had died, and I was supposed to protect my kids from harm. Well, I didn't; I was consumed with guilt and a sense of failure. I had failed my family miserably; I just wanted to run, but I couldn't. Everyone else was counting on me.

Jack had no skills for dealing with feelings. He had been socialized to maintain certain roles designated by society—those of stoic self-reliance. He didn't question whether it was right or wrong, he just did it.

The major problem is that the typical male role prescribed by our culture actually inhibits a father's successful resolution of grief. He is poorly equipped to deal with the loss of control that is such a monumental part of loss. He has never been taught how to react to vulnerability. When a major loss occurs, as it does throughout life, the average man reacts with anger and tight control over his emotions—until the taut rope holding him together snaps. He is left with serious feelings of failure and extreme loneliness.

Recognizing that men grieve differently from women, how could Jack have changed things sooner? Actually much needed to be changed before the loss even occurred. Yet, because so much of our role-dominated behavior is unconscious, it is often difficult to even recognize nonfunctional patterns until a crisis happens. Then our vulnerable selves are thrown open and we must consider the meaning of life. We must acknowledge an ending.

So, for Jack, one of the most freeing responses he could ever learn is that of letting go of so much control. You will hear this from me throughout this book, because I feel that taking responsibility (control) for other people's lives gets us into more trouble than any other one thing I know.

Jack needed to take care of himself and his own feelings before he was prepared to do this for anyone else.

As protector of the family, he needed to acknowledge the truth that he could not be there every minute to guard his family. And, very important, he needed to learn that he could not fix everything. In grief, we need to experience our pain, not have it removed—as if someone could. Allowing others to experience their own feelings and solve their own problems lets them learn competence and strength. Allowing others to be strong will help us free ourselves from negative roles.

The list that follows offers bereaved fathers suggestions that can provide a respite from extreme stress:

- Take some time for yourself. Go fishing, take long bike rides or walks in the woods, or spend a weekend or two alone at the beach. This allows time to eliminate distractions momentarily.

- Don't take on any new responsibilities. Give up some.

- Allow yourself to cry. This is a most healthy response because it not only lets out stored-up tensions, but it releases toxins from your body.

- Deal with your natural anger by venting on things, not people.

- Talk with other bereaved fathers and focus on *your* feelings—not how to help your wife. There is a good possibility that you need more help than she does.

- Talk with your wife about your feelings. Listen to her.

- Accept the fact that men grieve differently from women, and talk to your wife about this. Let her know your needs.

- Read about grief, the feelings and responses that you can expect to occur. Discuss what you read with other bereaved fathers.

- Take one day at a time. It's the only way.

The Grief of Mothers

For the most part, women are conditioned differently than men. Early on, a young girl is allowed, even encouraged, to express her feelings. She can cry without being made fun of. She can express fear openly, without being called "scaredy-cat" or "sissy." She can be affectionate with parents, siblings, and friends, without fearing that she'll be laughed at.

As she continues toward teenage years, she is given the typically feminine household tasks of washing dishes, helping with housework, and maybe even some ironing and cooking. In short, a girl is generally trained to nurture and care for a family of her own. Even if she is encouraged by her family to seek a career, she is nevertheless taught that she needs to have homemaking skills "just in case."

By the time she marries, a woman has usually developed the desire for a family. She is aware, although not totally, that children will represent an extension of herself. Having children is a rite of passage in which she will gain standing as a mature adult in the eyes of the community. She expects life to go on as she has planned, providing her a wonderfully secure place in her family. As a mother, she is the hub of the family wheel. Everything revolves around her.

If she should lose a child through death, her entire world is shattered.

Helen and Sam were a young couple who learned, when their daughter Jenny was in eighth grade, that she had a serious heart condition. She would eventually need a heart transplant, the doctors said.

Jenny had one sister, Susie, three years younger, who was born with Down's syndrome. Helen and Sam had given much time to working with Susie and had done a remarkable job in helping her surmount the obstacles of her birth defect. Susie was even going to public school —special classes, of course, but doing well.

When Jenny developed heart symptoms, it seemed impossible. Their perfect child. How could this be? Naturally, Helen devoted herself to taking care of Jenny as carefully as she had Susie. This put a heavy load on the marriage because Helen had to neglect almost everything else. Helen and Sam never had a minute for themselves. Besides, the extra financial strain weighed on Sam to the extent that he was working overtime every weekend.

By the time the medical team located a transplant and the operation was scheduled, both Sam and Helen were exhausted, worried, and distant. They both were giving all they had and getting nothing in return, in terms of nurturance.

The day of the operation was frightening. Jenny, before she was anesthetized, was consoling her parents, telling them she would be fine—and it would cure her heart trouble once and for all. She wouldn't be the heavy financial responsibility anymore. Helen broke down then, to think of her daughter taking care of them at such a time.

Helen has replayed this scene in her mind a million times since then. Jenny died before the operation was over. Helen was left with an all-consuming guilt. She remembered the times when her attention had gone solely to Susie. She agonized over the missed occasions to share things with Jenny. All she could see now was her own failure to be a good mother. In her shame at losing her perfect child, Helen viewed Jenny's death as a punishment from God.

Sam's reaction was as we would guess. He blamed the doctors, the health care system, his own inability to do anything about Jenny. He had no problem in venting his anger with close friends. This was a big help for him.

Because Helen was taught that it is wrong for a woman to show anger, she had no way to deal with her unconscious anger but to turn it on herself. She withdrew from Sam because of her self-loathing and because she didn't know how to receive nurturance. She had always given it. Her usual compassionate temperament changed to cool detachment, even with friends. After all, she had been supportive for so many others, and it had only brought her to this place of intense pain and unbearable sorrow.

Months went by. Sam couldn't understand why Helen didn't get a better grip on her emotions. She continued to cry every day. She remained withdrawn and was extremely moody.

Helen's healing was blocked because she couldn't verbalize her shame and guilt. Helen had never thought she had a problem talking about her feelings before, but in the past they had usually been the socially acceptable ones. Now Helen thought her feelings were too dark to share with anyone. The family that she had based her future on was sorely diminished. Hope, which had been such a motivating force for her life, was now gone.

Helen and Sam began therapy. She didn't want to go, she said later, but Sam kept insisting. Eventually, she poured out her self-denigration about being a terrible mother. She had to relate the negative memories over and over before she was ready to embrace the many positive ones. She needed to see how Susie adored Jenny, to realize that Helen had indeed helped to build a loving family relationship.

Slowly Helen released her anger and frustration at not being able to change things. Her courage and strength helped her to let go of the pent-up emotions and accept them as a valid part of herself.

The list that follows offers suggestions for bereaved mothers:

- Don't try to be perfect with your emotions. Feelings come in negative and positive amounts. Yours are simply yours, and you have a right to them. There is no perfect way to grieve.

- Take some time for yourself. Time alone is valuable; it gives you an opportunity to clear your mind. Go somewhere away from home, where negative memories don't cloud your emotions.

- Be kind to yourself. This is such a terribly painful period of your life. You need to bring small pleasures into your daily existence where possible.

- If months down the road you are still crying most of the time, try to discipline your emotional outpourings. Too much, too long has the effect of alienating everyone, leaving you unsupported. Don't shut off your emotions; just temper them slightly.

- Find support people and risk sharing your negative and shame-based feelings.

- Find support people so that you can continue to talk about your child. This is necessary for you to get a balance with your memories.

- Live one day at a time, and stop planning the outcome of things.

- Don't expect so much from yourself—or from anyone else for that matter. Expectations always lead to disappointments.

- Get more rest. Grief work takes as much out of you physically as hard labor. Take a nap in the afternoon or rest when you come home from your job. Try getting to bed earlier at night.

- Learn to use more assertive methods for releasing emotions. Note that I said "assertive," not aggressive. You can behave aggressively toward things, but if you use aggression with people, the consequences will never be what you want.

- Ask for what you need from husbands, bosses, children, and family; make sure you don't just sit back and expect them to do things. Again, expectations lead to disappointments. Let them all know what you need.

- Let go of control. We have no real control anyway, except within. Realize that a power greater than yourself can give you the strength to handle all your overwhelming feelings and negative thoughts. All you have to do is let them go. Things will work out.

- Because grief is a time of accelerated fears, acknowledge your anxieties. If you admit their presence, they will eventually leave—but only if you don't run from them.

EFFECT OF GRIEF ON THE MARRIAGE

A marriage that loses a child is seriously jeopardized. This seems strange in light of the fact that under most circumstances one spouse is the other's best friend. Therefore, we reason, my spouse should be there for me. We have just lost our child. We should cling to each other and gain strength from our mutual grief. But it doesn't happen that way. Because we are two unique individuals and because the child we have lost means different things to each of us, we will not be able to understand the other's position fully. Nor will we go through the phases of grief at the same time. One may still be in the withdrawal/conservation phase while the other may have moved on to healing. Your needs and tasks are not the same.

Gaining an accurate count of how many divorces happen because of the death of a child is difficult. So many divorces occur years after the death. But estimates suggest that anywhere from 50 to 75 percent of all marriages in which there has been child loss end in divorce. An even larger percentage of couples suffer discord and separation.

My marriage was one of the casualties. For six months prior to Jim's death, Hersh and I had been in a debate regarding Hersh's strictness with Jim. Looking back on it, I realize Hersh's excess discipline resulted from normal oedipal conflicts that enter into every father-son relationship when a boy reaches age sixteen or so. To me, at the time, it seemed like harsh cruelty—not physical abuse, but Hersh just seemed to be on Jim's back all the time. The issue had not been resolved when Jim was killed. From that point all the hostilities seemed crystallized, frozen in time.

Somewhere deep within me, I blamed Hersh. Withdrawing from him was easy. I had a heavy course load at college as well as my many other activities to tend to. It was easier to sit back and hate Hersh and myself than it was for me to admit hating what had happened to Jim. All of my insecurity at losing control of my world avalanched into that hate.

Hersh withdrew as well, but he never cried—not until I pointed out that he obviously didn't care. From then on our relationship was a standoff. We stopped speaking about Jim. My grief was personal; he wasn't included.

Hersh and I were in and out of therapy several times, going to only a few sessions on each attempt. Yet we stayed together and eventually started a Compassionate Friends group in Tampa. This helped us tremendously to verbalize our feelings. It was safer to do this with other parents who understood than it was with the counselors we had seen.

We built our friendship once again, slowly, with false starts and stops. Once the hatred was spent, we never gave up the deep caring we had for each other. But neither could we come together as partners again. The trust was damaged. We were divorced twenty years after Jim died.

As Harriet Sarnoff Schiff says in her well-received book *The Bereaved Parent,* "The most essential ingredient . . . in surviving well—besides facing reality—is to speak of the dead child unashamedly." For bereaved spouses, for bereaved families, I encourage open conversations about the child, about the spouses' own thoughts and emotions (including shame and anger), but most especially about their fears. We become frighteningly insecure in grief and fear that everything we know and love will be swept away, even ourselves. Only in hearing ourselves voice these thoughts out loud can we finally begin to free ourselves from the dark elements of grief.

To survive the heartaches of life, marriages must be built on trust. This requires total honesty. No secrets. Nowhere is this more important than when we are plunged into the despair of parental grief.

THE EFFECT OF GRIEF ON SIBLINGS

In open families, children will be supported in grief because their families give them permission and time to deal with the death. When parents share their feelings openly, the children learn that it is permissible to do the same thing. The children do not fear that they will be abandoned or rejected if their emotions are either excessive or minimized.

On the other hand, closed families are notoriously insensitive and rigid. Roles are carefully defined and provide little opportunity for appropriate grieving. Children are kept isolated and, as a result, feel doubly abandoned, first by their brother or sister, and next by their parents. So often extended family members and friends ignore the brothers and sisters of the dead child, reasoning that the siblings should be protected from something so painful. Or they think the children are incapable of grief. That is untrue. Protecting children from the reality of death is one of the greatest disservices we can do them.

Guilt seems to be the major negative emotion in sibling bereavement. Survivor guilt is a type that affects both siblings and parents alike. There is a distinct feeling among siblings and parents that they should have been the ones to die, that they are less worthy, less needed by the world and by the family than the lost child.

Children may feel responsible for the death. They might have been angry at the child before he died, wishing that he weren't around any more or saying typical childish things like "Drop dead" or "I wish I would never see you again." Then the brother or sister dies. The surviving child could carry enormous guilt if these thoughts are not verbalized to someone who understands.

The parents may expect the child to show more outward signs of grief than he or she does. This is particularly evident in adolescence, when young people often make a concentrated effort to suppress their grief. If the child detects that the parents disapprove of his or her lack of expression, the child may be burdened by guilt.

When the family is open, sharing memories together and hurting and crying together, guilt is avoided and grief work much less painful. Because parents give meaning to new and unfamiliar situations, children are powerfully influenced by their behavior. This is the way they learn, of course. When parents can offer appropriate explanations, tender interpretations of death, and their warm physical presence, the surviving children, whatever their ages, will benefit for a lifetime.

The list that follows offers suggestions for helping your remaining children:

- Be open, honest, and gentle in describing the death. Only offer details that the children can absorb. Don't overload.

- Have family powwows on a weekly basis or more often. Give each child a chance to talk.
- Give each child the opportunity to participate in devising meaningful family rituals.
- Check with each child to see if he or she is feeling guilt. Offer reassurance.
- Don't be afraid to let your child see you cry. They need to know that crying is a natural response.
- Be there for your children. They will need your affection and security now more than ever.

Family members trying to survive after the death of a child must truly pull together and remain open to each other. The gaping wound left by the child will be a raw and painful reminder that life isn't perfect. We have only this moment in time to count on. What becomes increasingly true is the need to focus on the blessings that are there in the remaining family unit. Nothing can ever replace the dead child. Grief teaches the importance of living one day at a time and recognizing that we are not in control of most things.

6

• • • • • • • • • • • •

Horrendous Deaths

THE WINDS howl at night. I think of last winter. I will never accept it—not like Daddy—which I knew would happen sometime. It is not a normal sorrow. Back of it is always, "It need not have happened." And that is a torture. I suppose I can only swallow it whole. It will not be absorbed, but will always be there, and always hurting, like something in your eyes. Nature does not absorb it but gradually provides a protective covering which numbs the sharp pain, but you are always conscious of it.

—Anne Morrow Lindbergh

Some will remember more vividly than others the terrible, nightmarish kidnapping and death of the Lindbergh baby. In the preceding passage, Anne Morrow Lindbergh writes poignantly of her painful thoughts surrounding that tragedy. Their son was kidnapped from the palatial Lindbergh home in New Jersey when she was there in another part of the house. A maid was supposed to be near him. When the nursery was checked later, all that was found was an open window and a ladder on which the kidnapper escaped from the second floor. No signs, no sounds.

The nation was stunned. That perfect family. Fame, fortune, glory. The name of Charles Lindbergh evoked patriotic pride in the hearts of all Americans. He was the first to fly the Atlantic, landing safely after hours all alone. He was our national hero. How could something so tragic happen to a family like the Lindbergh's? They were a private family, preferring to live with a large degree of anonymity. They simply wanted a peaceful place to raise their family. Instead, their privacy was invaded by a murderer who ripped their lives apart and left them publicly exposed forever.

Murder, suicide, fatal beatings, AIDs—all horrendous deaths. Too catastrophic to correlate with the innocence of children. These deaths are not children's events. These horrendous deaths, if they must happen at all, belong to the world of grown-ups—but, please God, not to children. And yet, we have only to pick up the daily newspaper or watch the news on TV to learn that these horrendous deaths are growing in number as causes of children's deaths.

Recently, in the *Los Angeles Times,* I read about one of the many gang slayings that are occurring more frequently among teenagers. In this case, a thirteen-year-old teenager had died while walking home from school, after being hit by a stray bullet fired by gang members. The murderer did not know him. He just aimed his semiautomatic and emptied it at a passing car, which he thought carried members of a rival gang. A senseless crime committed for no reason but to settle a gang's power struggle or supply a moment of excitement.

The victim was a well-liked, mannerly young man—a good student. He was described by friends as "a very sunny, down-to-earth child, a sweet person, very innocent." He wanted to become a police officer. He worked little jobs to raise money, bagging groceries at the Hillside Village Market and at Johnnie's Market. The owner of one of the markets helped collect money to pay for the boy's funeral.

How can the family and friends reconcile their grief? What comfort can be offered? They can, perhaps, find some small satisfaction when the offender is caught and punished. It will help ensure that the murderer won't do it again, at least for a while. But it won't explain the fate of their son, their friend. It will never bring their boy back again.

The article sickened me as I read it. All the protection this family had tried to arrange served little purpose in the end. He was gone. And they are left with emotions and thoughts too terrible to contemplate.

What terrors do these horrendous deaths leave with the survivors? How can they find peace when death has been so cruel, so violent? The amazing answer is that many parents, families, and friends actually do find eventual peace. Just how many, we do not know. There is very little data on the long-range outcome for these broken families. The death of a child is a parent's worst nightmare. A horrendous death compounds the nightmare.

MURDER

Murder violates everything we hold to be right. The very essence of all human values is that each individual has a right to life. When we come in contact with murder, whether directly as a family member or as a friend, neighbor, or bystander, we are thrown immediately into righteous indignation, screaming, "How could this happen?" A murder also evokes feelings of powerlessness and frustration, which can bring on anger, guilt, fear, and feelings of extreme vulnerability.

The violence of murder greatly complicates the shock effect of sudden death. The fact of a murder can't be believed. We can't fit it into our value systems. Research has shown that sudden death produces more intense grief reactions than death caused by chronic illness and that death by murder produces trauma that is even more long lasting and severe than that caused by an unexpected loss. When children are the victims of murder, grief is even more complicated. We can't imagine a child having to live through such torture. The chilling realization that a child was terrified, in agony and pain, alone and defenseless, fills us with helpless paralyzing rage. Our own pain temporarily cripples us. As parents, guilt at having survived our children's murders pervades our thoughts. But even beyond that is the terrible guilt of knowing that our children suffered and we were not there to prevent it.

Rick, twenty-one, was found floating in the bay in knee-deep water. His hands were tied behind his back. He had been shot once in the base of his brain. It was never known if there had been one or more persons involved. There was never a trial, never an explanation, never a just punishment for the murderers.

The hypothesis the police eventually offered was that Rick, who was out on his boat shrimping around 2:00 A.M., may have happened on a drug deal or some other illegal transaction. He became a witness who must be disposed of. Apparently, he was executed in typical gangland manner, on his knees, shot in the back of the head.

Rick had lived with his parents while he was completing his degree at the university. He was a quiet young man who spent time at home studying and working on his hobby of furniture building with his dad. The terrible irony of Rick's death was that it seemed he was the one on trial. At the beginning, the police believed that he was connected with a drug-smuggling operation. The family home became open shop for the police. They examined everything but uncovered nothing. The family's grief was ignored. It was months before the officials agreed that Rick had had nothing whatsoever to do with a drug exchange. He had simply been at the wrong place at the wrong time.

To Rick's father went the gruesome task of identifying his son's body. The shock from that experience set in motion a series of nightmares that continued for months. He would awaken in the middle of the night in a cold sweat. His anger was such that he began to plot the murderer's death, devising elaborate plans of torturous treatment so that the murderer would be made to suffer as his son had. He later said he became frightened of his own fantasies, but he kept quiet about them. As a consequence, he began staying to himself more and more, closing himself off to others for fear he would disclose these murderous impulses. He thought he was going crazy.

Rick's mother, a gentle loving woman, couldn't comprehend the violence of her son's death. Her initial reaction was disbelief—surely a mistake had been made. When the reality did sink in, she went through a constant rehearsal of the events. What happened? When? Where? Why her son? When she could finally take in some of the violence, she became afraid. She told me she was scared to leave her house without someone going with her. Her daughter, grandchildren, and husband were a constant source of concern for her now. What if something happened to them, too?

It is important to remember that these fears are not irrational. The death of a child by violence upsets the accepted order of life; to trust little or nothing for a long time is a natural response.

Rick's mother now takes comfort where she can. Sealed in a plastic bag she has a shirt that Rick especially liked. Whenever her longing becomes overpowering, she takes out the shirt (it still smells like him) and holds it close. This makes her feel momentarily as if she has Rick back with her again.

Rick's mother still suffers pangs of guilt because she didn't tell her son more often that she loved him.

> I was talking with my daughter about how sorry I was that I hadn't told Rick "I love you" enough, and she said, "Oh mom, you didn't have to tell him that. He knew how much you loved him. You showed it to him all the time." And I said, "Yes, I know," but all the same I'm sorry I didn't say it more than I did. I'm just sorry I didn't say it.

It is important to her that friends and neighbors, especially children, still take flowers to the cemetery. She doesn't feel that he is forgotten or that she is all alone in her grief.

Rick's mother often feels his presence. She can be out in the yard on a still day and suddenly feel a rush of cool air against her check and know, without a doubt, that it is Rick. It is a comforting experience, she says. Her faith in God is a comfort also.

> We just thank God that we have today and are thankful too that God gives us strength enough to take us through each day. It's tough and I miss him terribly, but with God's help, we'll get through.

Rick's father, on the other hand, feels his religious faith doesn't offer him the comfort that it does his wife. He's not sure about an afterlife or where his son is. Still, he endlessly pursues the search for some meaning in his tragic loss. His anger shows through as he rationalizes by saying that at least Rick is out of the turmoil of life.

I know he is out of the struggle of this world, which is terrible and getting worse. The country is in a mess, the politicians have taken all the money, and Lord knows what all. At least Rick is out of that, and he'll never have to contend with their mishandling of things.

But all the time Rick's father speaks wistfully, because he knows his son wanted to live and was full of life. Both parents agree that they wish they could have been the ones to die instead.

The aftermath of murder is rampant with fears and uncertainty for the parents of victims and those who wish to support them. Friends are perplexed and afraid to even approach the family. People turn away because of their own inadequacies and fear of saying the wrong thing. But these "murder victims," above all, must not be abandoned.

The Horror of Violence

Violence, except in the make-believe world of TV and films, isn't generally a part of our lives. We can't readily comprehend such an event as murder. When such a tragic event overtakes our child, we try to push the fact away. The reality doesn't makes sense. Nothing in our background prepares us for something so degrading and brutal. Our shock is interrupted by waves of nausea. "It can't have happened to my child. No, no, no. I will not accept this."

The trauma of violence and death forced upon our child stays with us for years—for a lifetime. The violence becomes a part of our lives, too, and we torture ourselves with the unanswerable: Why?

The Aftermath of Terror

All major losses leave us afraid. Fear is one of the prominent emotions we must deal with in grief. Following a murder, however, fear escalates into terror. Nothing is safe for us. If the murderer has not been caught, then our fear tells us that he is everywhere, lurking, waiting to strike again. Yet, even after the murderer has been apprehended, we are still terrorized. We now know that brutal slayings can and do happen. We are afraid to go out at night, afraid to leave even in the day, afraid to come home. We constantly fear that someone else in the family will be murdered. Our fears are rooted in our loss of faith in the world. If God would allow such a tragedy to occur, then I can never feel safe again anywhere.

It takes time for faith to regenerate after such a horrible crime has been committed. It is understandable that one is empty and fearful. But because fear is something we don't want to live with forever, we begin to re-establish our faith again and wait for our Higher Power to give us courage to trust.

Anger

Anger is also a natural part of all loss. We suffer at being deprived of the one we lose, and we are angered by our frustration. When the loss happens because of murder, we are struck with overwhelming rage. "This death did not need to happen" rings in our heads like a resounding clap of thunder. Our sheer helplessness increases our vulnerability. We feel out of control, unable to move or to effect a change. All of these responses are normal and to be expected.

Properly channeled, anger can provide an outlet for pent-up emotions that need to be released. Anger can provide energy when grief is draining our inner resources. It can provide us with temporary courage to keep on in the face of hopelessness.

It is only when our own murderous rage is acted out in violence of our own making that anger becomes destructive.

For that reason, it is necessary to have a support person or group to be there to allow some of the necessary ventilation. Search out others who will listen and not turn away from your anger. Only in the mirror provided by support people can we use our anger constructively. Having others be with our rage and not become afraid assures us that we have nothing to fear from our anger.

The Desire to Retaliate

The desire to "pay back" the murderer for all the pain caused by his or her senseless act is also quite normal. You want to see the murderer suffer just as he made your child suffer; just as he is making you suffer now. You create elaborate plans to inflict slow, agonizing deaths.

These retaliatory thoughts are scary. What if I'm going crazy? the grievers think. Often a sense of shame sweeps over the bereaved; they fear that, deep down inside them, they might be as bad as the murderer. This fear is yet another burden for the griever.

Like anger, murderous thoughts need to be verbalized. Harboring these negative but natural images keeps them fermenting deep inside, causing chronic grief and continuous unhappiness. In order to survive, we must find ways to normalize these images. Only then will they lose their strength.

Our Lives Become Public Property

Murder opens all the doors and bares the closets of the lives of the survivors. Nothing is private. At a time of enormous suffering, they must submit to the ceaseless questions of strangers, law-enforcement officers, reporters, attorneys, and others who are probing into the most personal matters in life. When there is a great need for privacy, there is none. The hardship of grievers goes unnoticed as professionals set about to do their jobs.

The trial places a further burden on the family. Besides the grueling days in the public courtroom, where the specifics of the crime are discussed with analytic detail, media makes public every aspect of the case. There is no place where the survivors can escape the horror of the death their loved one experienced. Their own grief must be put on hold until the case is decided in appeals and retrials. This can go on for years.

Empirical research shows that the families of murder victims are at risk of serious physical complications. The amount of trauma endured for such a long period of time leaves people with a reduced ability to fight infections or disease. These complications can also result in psychological distress: posttraumatic stress disorder (PTSD), in which nightmares, depression, inordinate fears, and inability to concentrate are prominent for a long time. These symptoms need to be treated.

Of all survivors, those whose children have been murdered need the most nurturance. They need professional psychotherapy to guide them through the trauma and ensure against either physical or psychological complications. They need safety so they can gradually regain some trust in the world. The list that follows offers suggestions for the families of murdered children:

- Make your home as physically secure as possible. Safety is important now.
- Find a support group as soon as possible. You need to have others near who can understand the overwhelming stress of murder.
- See a psychotherapist on a consistent basis. It is

important that you have a guide through this agonizing period.

- Draw near to your family. If you have a closed family, start a series of powwows. You all have much to verbalize, and it helps to start in the family. If discussions don't go well, pull a family therapist in to moderate.
- Verbalize your anger.

SUICIDE

She was a lovely college junior with chestnut brown hair and penetrating blue eyes. Yet Cassy Edwards seemed to be having trouble in every area of her life: family, school, and now she was having problems with a serious relationship. No part of life seemed to be bringing any satisfaction. She confided in a classmate during a serious discussion in her apartment one night:

> I thought by now I'd have all my problems worked out— well a lot of them, anyhow. I thought, surely, things would get easier for me. They've gotten worse. I couldn't find my way back to the beginning even if I could figure it all out. . . . Oh well, what the heck. What choice do I have?

Cassy had been brought up in an upper–middle-class family and had been given all the material things children want and wish for. Her parents and siblings were intelligent, educated, and charming. She had an older brother, her mother's favorite, and a younger sister, her father's little girl. Cassy struggled for approval from her parents constantly—sometimes got it, sometimes didn't. Whatever, Cassy never felt she measured up in the eyes of her talented and popular parents.

Cassy had wanted desperately to go away to college. She felt that, if she could get away from the constant pressure of family, she would be independently happy. She could really be herself. Cassy had determined this with the help of a counselor she saw while she was in high school. And it had worked that way in the beginning.

By her sophomore year, she was in love. For the first time she had someone who loved her, too—just her. This was truly the happiest time of her life. Unfortunately, it didn't last. Cassy took Bill home one weekend in October, thrilled to show him off to her family. But what she expected to be total approval ended in dismal failure. Cassy, who read her parents with amazing accuracy, sensed their polite disapproval. She was crushed but determined not to let them make a difference in her love for Bill.

However, years of working on pleasing her parents set a habit hard to break. Little things about Bill began to annoy her. She was irritable with classmates. Her grades began to slip. She would have times with Bill that were like the beginning—happy and carefree—but they grew further apart.

They took a break from each other during the holidays to think things through. Cassy kept to herself most of the time, angry at her parents, angry at herself for not having strength to stand up for her own happiness. By the time she was ready to return to school, she was sure of what she wanted. She truly wanted to spend her life with this wonderful young man who loved her. She wrote all this to Bill the week before classes were to begin.

Bill answered by return mail. Shocked and dismayed, Cassy read his letter. He didn't want to continue the relationship. During the holidays, he wrote, he had rekindled a love he had had with a girl in his hometown and now felt really happy with her. He told her they would never have made it with her parents feeling as they did about him. Cassy was devastated. It was true. Nothing worked out for her.

Mr. and Mrs. Edwards were both home on that Saturday afternoon when the police car drove up. The officer apologized for bringing bad news. Cassy was dead. Their daughter had shot herself in the head early that afternoon as she sat in her car in a nearby park. Her note simply said: "Things will never turn out right for me."

Reports estimate that 5,000 people age twenty-four and under killed themselves in 1988. This estimate is probably low because many families conceal a child's suicide. It is too painful to admit to. But we know for a fact that in the last thirty years the rate of reported suicides among young people has nearly tripled. It may be shocking to realize that suicide, after accidents, is the leading cause of death among fifteen- to nineteen-year olds.

Guilt

As rage and terror are representative of families of murder victims, guilt and shame are the hallmarks of families whose children have taken their own lives. The question Why? pervades the minds of the parents, relatives, and friends. Yet, for parents and siblings, there is underlying torment. I surely could have done something; I could have stopped it, they think. Blame of one's self is rampant. What was it that I did or said that could have caused such misery? What did I leave undone? What could I have done to change things? Maybe I was too strict. On the other hand, maybe if I had provided more guidelines for behavior, she would have felt more secure. Mary, a bereaved mother whose eleven-year-old son hanged himself, said:

> Tommy's death is inconceivable. How was it that I didn't see . . . oh my God, why couldn't I see his unhappiness? I can only torture myself now with the questions. I can't find any answers. This is horrible . . . it is horrible. I'll always blame myself.

As parents, we undertake the responsibility to give life and a future to our children. When a child decides that he or she doesn't want this gift, it is the ultimate rejection. We have failed to provide a safe and secure environment. We have failed to give even happiness. We have failed everything. This terrible sense of failure and rejection stems in part from the powerlessness we feel at not being able to change anything. Though this feeling results no matter how a child dies, it is stronger when we convince ourselves that we could have changed the situation.

Stigma

When a child commits suicide, we not only feel that we have failed that child, but we also feel the shame at failing our community. We have not lived up to the silent promise we made to be responsible parents and protect our children.

Society, on the other hand, promotes this notion by avoiding parents of children who die by suicide. Studies have shown that these parents are liked less, blamed more, and viewed as more disturbed than parents of children who have died from other causes. No wonder these parents live with such guilt and shame. Just at a time when they need community support, there is instead the added stress of community isolation.

Punishment

Along with the deep feelings of rejection that bereaved parents feel after a loss by suicide, they also feel that their children have punished them, openly and forever. Not only must they face this anguish alone and unattended by society, but they must somehow manage to grieve the sorrow and the loneliness for their children alone too. With this much isolation, it is not unusual for parents and family members to direct anger at their children for their "irresponsible and malicious" act. This is done usually when the despair is momentarily forgotten. It is a very normal emotion and never should be the cause of self-condemnation.

The parents and families of children who die by suicide suffer a long and difficult bereavement. One of the hardest tasks is to learn to forgive themselves. There must always be this gentle reminder: "I did the best I could, given the circumstances." We don't always have the right answers and hindsight is keener than current knowledge. When we condemn ourselves, however, we are trying to control the situation. Of course, this is impossible. The only way to peace is in forgiveness. It does not come quickly or easily, but it is always possible. The list that follows offers suggestions for the families of suicides:

- Work toward forgiving yourself.
- Seek out support groups such as Survivors of Suicide, whose members can listen nonjudgmentally as you talk of your guilt, anger, and sorrow. They have been there and they know.
- Talk to a counselor trained in working with families of suicides.
- Talk to others about the death. It is important that you continue to replay all the memories you have. If people change the subject, gently ask them to listen. Explain that talking is vital to resolution.

ACQUIRED IMMUNE DEFICIENCY SYNDROME (AIDS)

It will be hard to forget Ryan White, the eighteen-year-old boy who died from AIDS in the spring of 1991. He became a national figure at age thirteen as he fought to attend public school. The school had barred him from classes for fear he would contaminate other children. From that he suffered greatly. Hatred and abuse were directed toward Ryan and his family by the residents of their town, where they were isolated and alienated.

Ryan was a hemophiliac who had contracted AIDS through a contaminated blood product. He won a landmark court case to attend school, but family members, by that time, had decided it would be too painful to stay on in a community where no one wanted them. They later moved to a nearby town where the family was made to feel welcome and wanted. Ryan was a junior in high school when he died. He had suffered with AIDS for 5½ years.

Of all the horrendous deaths of the present day, AIDS is the most stigmatic. Families of AIDS victims are avoided, alienated, and shunned more than any other bereaved persons. AIDS has been called a modern-day leprosy of epidemic proportions. Because the disease was originally confined to gay men and intravenous drug users, it hasn't been thought of as affecting children. Lately, however, we are beginning to be aware of the number of infants who are born with AIDS from infected mothers and children who have been infected by blood transfusions or contact with infected adults. The number of AIDS cases in adolescents and young adults is growing even more rapidly than the number of cases in younger children.

Another widely reported AIDS story involved a five-year-old boy who was barred from Sunday school because he had AIDS. Church officials were afraid that AIDS could be passed on through saliva. Even though there had never been a documented case in the United States where AIDS had been spread in this way, fear and lack of education predominated. The boy was later allowed to attend Sunday school, but I can't help but wonder how much that child had to suffer in terms of loneliness and degradation.

Then there was Kim Bergalis, the young woman who was infected with AIDS by her dentist. Kim was a young college student who planned to graduate from college, become an actuary, marry, and have children. That is the dream we are promised in life as we grow up—a chance to lead a normal happy life. "Nothing was going to stop those plans," she said.

Before she died, Kim addressed lawmakers: "I'd like to say that AIDS is a terrible disease that you must take seriously . . . I did nothing wrong, yet I'm being made to suffer like this. My life has been taken away."

These cases are ones that have made the news and have generated much public support for the victims and their families. But thousands of other AIDS victims and their families suffer in shame and silence.

The stigma of AIDS is based on fear and lack of knowledge. Certainly, in the case of AIDS, there is much to fear. Even though it is a new lethal disease, first seen in 1978, reports estimate that more that 1½ million people in the United States are infected. There is no known cure, and death comes slowly and painfully. Nevertheless, no one, child or adult, should have to suffer the stigma of this disease in addition to the awful pain and disintegration that accompanies it. Yet, it is well-documented that when families, parents, and victims are isolated, shamed, and disgraced, the effect becomes analogous to that of ousting of the members from the community. Just at a time when a child is ill and dying, those in support systems often turn their backs.

The three horrendous deaths discussed in this chapter —murder, suicide, and AIDS—frighten us all. We recoil in terror at the violence that surrounds them. In an attempt to hide from our fears, we tend to shun the families of these victims. Just when it is imperative that bereaved families be nurtured and supported, the alienation we cause increases their fears.

Because these horrendous deaths are on the increase, it is important that we try to look beyond our fears and reach out to grieving families. We all need each other— desperately at times. Taking care to "be there" for our neighbors ensures that our neighbors will be there for us when we need them. It's the only way we can manage horrendous grief.

7

• • • • • • • • • • • • • •

Loss of the Unborn and Newly Born

I HAD only been home from the hospital for a couple of hours and my next-door neighbor came. She hadn't any more stepped in the door when it hit me. I thought, "My God, she brought her baby!" I just remember seeing that baby and thinking, "How could you? You know mine has just died."

—Bereaved mother, age 26

When a pregnancy ends—regardless of whether it ends in miscarriage, stillbirth, or infancy—the parent's expectations are cruelly dashed. Hopes and dreams are lost when the wished-for child dies. For a number of reasons a baby's death is particularly hard to sustain. The baby is so helpless, so dependent on us to carry him or her through to maturity. Parents feel especially responsible for what has happened; angry that it should have happened to them; guilty that somewhere, somehow, they may have been the cause. In cases of prebirth loss, mothers are often angry with their bodies' betrayal.

In addition, the loss of the future is hard to accept. The parents will never get to know this child. The special firsts in a lifetime never come: the first Christmas, the first steps, the first day of school, graduation. When the baby dies before birth, parents are left with few reminders that they ever were. For these parents, rituals are often denied or minimized.

The loss does not affect the community, so there is little support for the parents. Many friends and relatives even ignore the death. They have a hard time imagining your grief over a baby you never saw or held only briefly. Many feel as if, for grief to be valid, we must have years to establish a relationship.

But prebirth and infant losses are real. The relationship between parents and child often begins before conception. If the parents loved and wanted that child, they have a right to their grief. They have an equal right to be supported through their grief, whatever it takes.

MISCARRIAGE

Whether the baby was expected or not, wanted or reluctantly accepted, when pregnancy terminates early, there are changes to deal with. The emotional effect of miscarriage is grossly misunderstood. The fact that it happens every year to approximately 800,000 families in this country would lead to the expectation that there would be more support when it occurs. Instead, our society tends to minimize and overlook the effects of miscarriage because the loss happens so early in the pregnancy. In reality, the reactions vary widely among individuals. These symptoms can range from complete acceptance to inner turmoil, isolation, and depression. Many parents need psychological help when the symptoms are severe. Much depends on the individual circumstances surrounding the miscarriage.

When Karen came to and realized she was in a hospital bed, she immediately tried to feel her stomach to see if she had lost her baby. She couldn't move her right arm. Karen tried the other one and slowly moved it toward her stomach. There were bandages across her abdomen. Had they taken the baby? she thought. She was aware of excruciating pain everywhere in her body. Groggily, she tried to lift her head and see what had happened to her, but she was unable to move it.

What happened? Where's my baby? Her thoughts were a confused jumble, and she could resurrect no immediate memories. How did I get here? Oh God, I hurt. She blacked out again.

What Karen White didn't know at that time was that she had been in a serious car accident. Driving alone, she was on her way to see her doctor for a normal checkup. She was 4½ months pregnant. Another car had run a red light and hit her on the driver's side.

The other driver was treated and released. Karen suffered severe multiple injuries when her car door caved in, shattering her left hip; breaking her left leg and right arm; and, sadly, killing her baby. A hysterectomy was performed because of damage in the pelvic area.

Karen and Joe White had been married for ten years. They both had careers they wanted to develop and so they delayed parenthood. By the time Karen was thirty-four,

both she and Joe felt they were in a good position to start
their family. They had no argument concerning a desire
for three children. Nor did they concern themselves with
what sex they would prefer. "Just healthy babies," Karen
often said. "We can now give them advantages we didn't
have."

In the hospital, when she woke up again, Joe was there.
It hurt too much to move, even form words, but she was
frantic enough to say weakly, "Baby?"

Joe had never been good at hiding anything from
Karen. She could always read him. When he didn't immediately reassure her, she knew something was wrong.
Oh, God . . . not my little baby. . . . Surely she's okay. She
has to be okay. Karen's thoughts were coming slowly,
painfully, as she tried to make sense out of everything.
It seemed as if she were trying to move through waist-
deep water.

"What . . . happened?" Joe began to tell her about the
accident. She remembered nothing. She remembered getting dressed for her appointment with Dr. Crane, but that
was all. Joe told her how the accident had happened,
the extent of her injuries and that she had been in the
hospital four days now. "The baby didn't make it, hon.
God, I'm so sorry. For a while, we didn't think you would
either."

Tears began to streak Karen's face as she tried to comprehend what he had told her. Oh God, I've lost my baby
was all that she could process. Nothing else mattered.

There was more sadness to come, however, as she learned
over the next few weeks in the hospital that she had
not only lost her baby, but would never be able to have
any others. Her hopes, built during the years of planning
for her family, were dashed. Everything suddenly seemed
very empty.

Karen immediately turned all her grief inward, blaming herself for being a murderer. The physical pain
she suffered seemed only right, as some kind of awful

punishment. She didn't care if she recovered or not. Nothing mattered—not her, not Joe, not their marriage.

Joe was saddened at the loss too. Yet he had been able to see the unborn baby after she had died. He was even permitted to hold her for a moment. This helped tremendously, he said, because at least he knew that she had been. His grief for his daughter was lessened by his worry over Karen. She had lost so much—her baby, her ability to have other children—there was even a question if she would walk again without the use of a cane or walker.

Karen was tightly focused on the fact that she had never even seen her baby, much less held her. There were no pictures, no evidence to Karen that her daughter had ever been. She had no memories to hold up of her one and only child. Having no concrete reminders of her baby made her loss especially difficult to acknowledge.

Karen needed to process every aspect of her pregnancy: her hopes for her child, the ultrasound session when she and Joe first learned that the baby was a girl, the names they pondered and the one they chose. The wish for a future with her child had to be reviewed and let go. She also needed to review and release her wishes for the other children she had planned to have and now couldn't.

The guilt at having "caused" the baby's death was difficult for her to release. Karen became so used to thinking of this loss as "her failure" that for months she found reasons to keep the guilt alive. For a time she even anguished over whether she had really had the right of way in the accident or not. At one point she lamented, "Sarah was only in her fourth month, and already I couldn't take good care of her. What kind of mother would I have been anyhow?"

Going home from the hospital was another ordeal. Her sense of guilt and failure escalated as she walked out the hospital door with empty hands, nothing to show for her months of pregnancy. Her family was focused on her physical well-being. Later she angrily noted, "Not one person mentioned the baby to me." Instead there were comments like "You are lucky to be alive" and "How wonderful that you are out of such horrible pain now." She said to me, "I could have killed them. I was furious. Imagine saying I was out of pain. What do they know about pain? Not one person there knew how awful it was for me to be without my child. Not one person even cared about her."

When others don't acknowledge our grief, it becomes almost necessary to mourn twice as much just to make up for their lack of understanding. Adding bitterness and anger to her deeply lodged guilt, Karen had to deal with the shattering disappointment of never having children. She railed against the doctors, nurses, any hospital staff member she could think of until the anger was finally spent inside her. All the control she had used in determining when and how she would have her babies was of no use to her now. She had to learn that there was never any control there anyway. She had only thought so. Because she could vent her anger in some direction other than toward herself, she could finally release the illusion of control and begin to live one day at a time.

When Karen was able, I suggested a support group for couples who had suffered a miscarriage. This was a wonderful help for Karen and Joe because they could finally process their grief with others who had experienced a similar event. Their work in the support group was a healthy step for them with their marriage, also. They were able to talk about issues that related to their feelings for one another. Keeping the communication open got them through that tragic period of their life.

Miscarriage is poorly recognized by others as a real cause for grief, especially if the pregnancy ends in the early months. For the mother, it is the beginning of her child's life. Yet, in most cases, she never sees the fetus. She mourns alone. In some situations, no one else in her daily life even knows that she was pregnant. Guilt occurs as the mother blames herself for her failure (as she sees it) to produce a healthy baby. Anger generally turns inward unless there is an external cause for miscarriage. Even then, the mother will find something for which to blame herself. The internally directed anger will result in depression unless the mother is able to process it with a supportive person or group. Until she can reduce her anger and guilt, grief will be slow to resolve.

INDUCED ABORTION

Pregnancies are not always wanted. Sometimes the decision to terminate is brought on by social or financial circumstances and represents hours of agonizing conflict. Abortion may be the only solution that seems appropriate at the time.

Even though legal abortion has been practiced for some time in many states, there is still a great deal of shame, stigma, and secrecy surrounding this procedure. Even actively pro-choice women may feel a deep sense of guilt.

For many women, an abortion is coupled with the breakup of a relationship, and this causes even deeper loss and sadness. The woman must then go through the procedure alone and without support. Finding oneself alone and pregnant, one is supposed to accept the "out" of an abortion with relief. The denial of grief runs high in these cases as mothers, fathers, and friends put pressure on her to "get it over with."

However, I have seen many middle-aged women in therapy finally ready to mourn the lost baby after years of putting it out of their minds. The anger and guilt back up until they overflow into conscious awareness. Often the woman is totally dismayed to have such volatile feelings appear after such a long period of time. In the case of Betty and Sean, we can see a real cause for anger.

Betty had been going with Sean for about seven months. Though they had never talked about marriage, there had been a strong understanding by Betty that the relationship would lead to marriage. There had already been some talk of Sean moving in with Betty, since she had the larger apartment. They got along well except for the times when Sean drank too much. Then he tended to become argumentative and extremely independent. Once he left Betty at a nightclub to get home as best she could. Betty later forgave him when he meekly asked her to take him back.

When she missed two menstrual periods, she bought a pregnancy test. She didn't tell Sean. Why say anything if she wasn't sure? But the test showed a positive result. She called her doctor and saw her the next day. It was confirmed. Betty was pregnant.

She was secretly happy because she felt that this would help them speed up the marriage. She expected Sean to react in the same happy way. That was not the response she got, however. Instead, Sean was shocked. He couldn't say anything at first. When he did speak, his first words were not, "We'll work this out together" or anything like that. Instead, Sean's first words were "You'll have to get an abortion. I won't be responsible for a baby." Angrily, he left.

Betty talked with him on the phone a few times after that, but he stood firm. He was through with the relationship. Sean blamed Betty for trying to trap him and emphatically stated he had no intentions of settling down yet.

At first, Betty was determined not to get an abortion. She felt betrayed by Sean, humiliated, and shamed. Her anger prompted another reaction, however. The angrier she became at Sean, the more she began to feel ambivalent about having his baby.

She agonized over what her parents would think of their pregnant daughter or how she would face her colleagues at work. The breakup alone was humiliating but to then go through the pregnancy alone, take care of a baby alone, and support a baby alone was more than she could do. Nevertheless, she was opposed to abortion unless it was medically necessary. The conflicts grew. As yet she had told only her best friend, living in another state, who urged her to go ahead with the abortion.

There wasn't much time left to have it done. Betty was already 2½ months pregnant. She had to make a decision. After weighing all the alternatives, she decided abortion was the only possible solution.

Betty rationalized to herself: "It was the only thing I could do." But she felt awful. She couldn't shake the anger that she now turned on herself. Her self-esteem was low, and she began to keep to herself. No one at work knew, which was good. But because of the secrecy, there was no one to give her encouragement, either.

In the beginning she felt little guilt about the abortion. That came later. It was not until about six months later, as she approached the time when the baby would have been born, that she began grieving. She found herself staring at every baby she saw, wondering if hers would have been like that. She began to search her life for deeper meaning, trying to locate a reason for all that had happened to her. She felt anxious, irritable, and weepy. She longed for a trusting relationship.

Betty had to deal with two significant losses, her pregnancy and a significant relationship. She received no support for her grief. Instead, she was left alone to sift through all the conflicts associated with her broken relationship and lost baby. It didn't help her to say Sean was not worth having. The fact is, Betty felt alone and empty.

It took her a long time to share her story with a therapist and work through the negative feelings about herself. Her hardest task was forgiving herself. The next hardest was to let her baby go—to give up all her fantasies about how the baby would look, how it would act, or how Betty would be as a mother. When she could forgive herself, a certain level of trust returned to her, and she was able to put that trust into others once again.

STILLBIRTH

Unlike induced abortion, in stillbirth the loss is not the desired solution. Death may come suddenly, without warning. One day the mother notes the usual signs of life within her and after that, quietness. When the worst fear is verified by ultrasound or stethoscope, the shock can be devastating.

Many times, stillbirth occurs for older couples, for whom the likelihood of birth anomalies is higher than for younger couples. In these cases, with time limits imposing a serious threat, the pregnancy might be their last chance at having a child. When the baby is stillborn, the entire grief process is escalated.

The awareness of problems with the pregnancy may come suddenly or with forewarning. For Judy the warning came in November, when the first amniocentesis was performed. In this procedure amniotic fluid is drawn from the mother to detect a congenital abnormality or negative intrauterine event. The test is usually done for women over thirty-five or for younger women with a history of miscarriage. Judy had already gone through three miscarriages of undetermined cause, but they had all occurred around two months. She was now thirty-six and 4½ months pregnant. Needless to say, she and Roger were thrilled, thinking that they were over the hurdle.

The amniocentesis did not go well. To the surprise of all, there was no amniotic fluid to draw. This fluid is actually the urine of the fetus and is necessary for lung development. A fetus may be able to survive in utero without fluid, but cannot live once born, because the lungs have not developed. For some reason, the fetus had not begun to produce amniotic fluid. The doctor told them there was a slight chance that the fluid could still come. They needed to wait another month.

Judy felt betrayed. She had so many hopes for this pregnancy. How had she gotten past the first trimester if something was wrong? Why let her go on hoping even for a day if their baby wasn't going to live? She had been so careful—had cut out all alcohol, eaten only the right food, continued her exercise program, and even started working only part-time to ensure her rest. What more could she do?

Judy still clung to the hope that the fluid would come. She knew it would not help matters to think negatively, so she tried to put all those answerless questions out of her head. Everything would work out, she tried to believe. Judy and Roger went through the holidays with many dips in mood. They continued to hope and plan for the baby's arrival. They chose a name to have ready at the birth: Kirk.

Their faith was strong as they returned from spending Christmas holidays with Judy's family. Having received much support from the family, they felt more assured than ever that little Kirk would be born in April. A perfect little baby. The second amnio was scheduled in early January. Judy and Roger were nervous as they drove to the office that day. So much hinged on a good report.

But there wasn't a good report. There was still no fluid. Later tests showed that the fetus's kidneys were multicystic and that there were equally severe midline deformities. The doctor said Judy might be able to carry the baby to term, but the baby absolutely could not live.

The awful decision-making process Judy and Roger agonized over lasted only a day or two. How could they let the baby live to term and then die? If it had to happen, they thought, the sooner the better. They decided to terminate the pregnancy.

Everyone congratulated them on making the right decision. Inside, however, Judy felt she was slowly dying. She had wanted this baby so desperately. It seemed like her very last chance.

They scheduled the "delivery" for the next day. Judy cried all night as she rubbed her swollen belly, trying to comfort her tiny baby still alive within her. She felt like a murderer, robbing her baby of his life. But she imagined the dry womb to be an even deadlier place. She knew her choice was really no choice at all. Without realizing it, Judy and Roger had already begun the grief process, of letting go, of giving up this longed-for child.

Labor was induced and the waiting began. When contractions began, they were very painful. As Judy said, "It's one thing to go through labor and end up with a healthy baby. It's another thing to go through all this for nothing. It doesn't make sense."

Six hours passed. The fetal monitor indicated that the baby was still alive. Judy and Roger shared a terrible fear then that he might be born alive. They didn't think they could bear seeing him die in front of their eyes.

They waited—two more hours—contractions getting more severe, coming more often. Roger was helping Judy breathe when suddenly, in the midst of excruciating pain, the baby's head showed. Kirk was born—dead.

The doctor wrapped him in a blanket and gently laid him in Judy's arms. Judy and Roger sobbed as they looked into his beautiful little face and saw Roger's chin and Judy's nose—a perfect composite of the two of them.

The hospital staff were wonderfully caring and sensitive. They let Judy and Roger be with their son for as long as the couple needed. It was two hours before they gave their baby back to the nurses. Judy was moved to another room in the hospital.

They said later that seeing their baby helped in two important ways. They were able to see their child as part of themselves, a tangible love object, and they were then able to say goodbye—to begin to let him go. These two processes were necessary in dealing with their grief. This does not mean that there wasn't deep pain connected with both events. Judy suffered intense yearning for her baby for months. She had periods of wanting to see him, touch him, talk to him. It was especially hard because she and Roger had so few concrete reminders of Kirk—a tiny box with his ashes, a death certificate, a little photo was all the evidence they had that he had really ever existed.

Grief continued for some time for Judy and Roger, especially as they realized there would probably not be another chance for Judy to bear their wished-for child. This realization was confirmed seven months later, when Judy miscarried again.

There was much to reconcile: their anger, especially Judy's anger at her body that had failed her, and their guilt. Judy felt guilty that somewhere, somehow, she had caused the tragedy. Roger felt guilty because he couldn't fix it all. They both yearned for Kirk, and they endured much sadness because he did not have a chance at life.

Some friends made their grief more difficult by ignoring their grief or minimizing it. These friends said things like, "It was good that you knew this ahead so you could do something about it," or "Don't worry, you can have other children," or "At least you didn't know the baby."

Stillbirth is an extremely painful experience. The high hopes of the pregnancy are dashed with disappointment and grief. There is very little social support for the parents after the event. Rarely does anyone think about the fact that the baby was real and had been fantasized about just as if it had lived. Little Kirk had been planned for and was intensely grieved after he died.

Judy and Roger have since adopted a baby boy. Judy said that not until their son came was she able to finally stop grieving Kirk's death.

NEONATAL DEATH

There are times when pregnancy goes to term without a problem of any kind. A normal delivery takes place. Everything goes well up to a point. Then suddenly the infant develops complications. He or she grows worse. The parents may or may not realize their newborn has a life-threatening condition until the baby dies. The shock and disbelief they experience parallel those felt by all grieving people following a sudden death. Nothing has prepared the parents for this unexpected loss. The parents frantically seek explanations from the medical staff. The caregivers who are the most helpful are those who recognize the need to be nurturing and kind while at the same time answer questions as honestly and completely as possible. Because guilt is such a predominant reaction in child death, helping the parents to realize that they did not cause the death is immensely important. The caregivers, at the same time, can play a significant role by acknowledging the parents' right to grieve as well as giving permission for the parents to grieve openly. Caregivers and parents should always refer to the infant by name, thus supporting the reality of the life. These steps will help the parents normalize their loss—that is, to experience grief as a painful but surmountable process rather than an enduring pathological state.

Because the infant may have been in the intensive care unit (ICU), the parents possibly did not have an opportunity to hold their baby, to bond with the baby before he or she died. There will be a deep sadness and intense longing to do this after the death. Many times the mother has been confined to the hospital room and couldn't get to ICU. The father was the only one who could see or touch the child before death. In these cases, because of the active participation, the father is helped through his grief more than he would have been if he had acted only as strong supporter. Often, the hospital quickly moves the mother off the maternity unit. In the case of Pat, whose baby died at five days, it was not the best decision.

And I said, "Why do I want to be moved off the floor?" I mean, I know this happens to people. I'm just not that kind of person to be bitter. Heck, my best friend has a little kid a year old and my other friend that I went to visit has one 2½ months. Why should I feel deprived or anything? I don't know what I feel. I think my hormones still are not synchronized, you know what I mean? Sometimes I feel really low, but there's no need to move me. That would make me feel worse—like I hadn't even had a baby.

Pat was stuggling to be rational at a time when there's no rationality. The death had happened so quickly.

The doctor told me on the fourth day, "He can go home with you," and then four hours later he came in and said the baby had developed serious problems. I really only actually held him twice. From that point on he was all hooked up, and everything went from bad to worse. About a day later, he died. So I really didn't have that much time to spend with him.

Pat told me that she wished her doctor had been more forthright in telling her the prognosis. She said that she would have liked him to say her baby's chances weren't good. But instead, she had to try to figure things out for herself.

When I went up to see him the night before he died, I could see he was in trouble. I noticed the oxygen level was up to 100%, so I knew he wasn't breathing on his own. I remember saying "This isn't good is it?" And then he died about four hours later. So even if the doctor wouldn't tell me, I knew things had gotten pretty bad.

Pat regrets that she wasn't able to attend the burial service. As it turned out, she had to remain bedridden for several weeks at her parents' home. One good thing about that, she said, was that it allowed her time to get used to the fact that their child would not be going home with them. She and John have only a few reminders of their baby, yet they do have a memory of being with him and holding him that remains very precious to them. They have since given away the clothes they had for him and have only kept the crib and changing table. Those are in the attic awaiting another day, when a little sister or brother will use them. Until then, they don't want to lose the image of that precious boy they had for only a few days.

John said later that the experience had caused a tremendous change within himself:

> I went from an all-time high—watching our child being born—to an all-time low—watching him die. It put a lot of things in a different perspective. I used to get upset over a lot of things—really frazzled. But now when something comes up I say, "Man, this is not important enough to get myself worked up about. After you have gone through a death, you realize there are so many things that are so unimportant . . . work, getting things in on a deadline—well, they may be important to the company, but if something isn't done it's not the end of the world. I would have never thought this way before our baby died.

SUDDEN INFANT DEATH SYNDROME (SIDS)

SIDS is the most frequent cause of all deaths occurring during the first year of life. Sudden infant death syndrome, or crib death, is the sudden unexpected death of an infant who has been well and shows no observable cause for death. The death remains unexplained even after autopsy. Most SIDS deaths happen between midnight and nine in the morning and are the cause of eight to ten thousand deaths a year in the United States. The suddenness and mystery attached to it create a grief filled with shock and agony as well as deep underlying guilt. The entire family constellation is affected by this tragic loss.

Rita and Sam Ellis were a young couple who had recently moved to a new community. Sam was a chemistry professor at the university and Rita was taking some time off from her teaching career to be with their new six-month-old daughter, Judy. Moving in August, they arrived just in time for Sam to begin teaching his classes. They had enjoyed a beautiful fall, getting acquainted with new friends and the community; by Christmas they felt settled in. Rita's parents spent some of the holidays with them, spoiling Judy with abundant love. She was the center of their attention, of course. Judy was a little blond angel who was responsive to them all. The whole family adored her.

The new year started with great promise. Sam had come home with the news that he would most likely be selected for tenure, so they could feel this community was home. He and Rita went to bed on a high note. Judy got her usual 2:00 A.M. bottle and then went back to sleep.

Rita's first thought that morning when she woke was "Wonderful, Judy let us sleep in a little later than usual." She tiptoed in to see if Judy was awake. The minute she stepped into the room, she knew something was wrong. Judy was on her stomach, perfectly still—too still. Rita rushed to her and picked her up. Judy's little body was ice-cold. Rita couldn't stop screaming. John called 911, then the doctor, then a neighbor who was a nurse. Nothing could be done. Judy was dead. Rita said later,

I don't even remember people being there. I held Judy close to give her my body heat. I remember thinking this couldn't be happening—not for real. I must be having a nightmare. But then something would happen that would jerk me back, like the police arriving. I do remember them, I remember thinking Oh God, they think I killed her! Someone tried to take Judy from me, and I screamed at them to leave me alone. It was all so horrible. Eventually, I had to let her go.

They got through the funeral somehow. Those first days were like a continuation of the nightmare Rita had experienced when she first found Judy. Nothing made any sense. Both she and Sam searched their memories for clues that would solve the awful mystery. Why did Judy die? This just doesn't happen to good people. No answers.

The next months were hard on Rita. Her anguish at being separated from her baby was more than she could bear. Rita had spent so much time with Judy. Now her preoccupation with thoughts and memories was overpowering. She heard Judy's cries, actually saw her image, dreamed about her, searched the house for her things. This led to angry frustration when nothing she did brought Judy back.

As a response to her angry outbursts, Rita began to blame herself more and more. She went over everything that she had done for Judy, searching for anything that was different from the usual. She would question Sam until he would grow angry, stating that there was nothing she had done to cause Judy's death. She would argue that he must blame her. He would try to reassure her that he didn't.

Sam dealt with his grief in a different manner. Through the entire ordeal, he acted as protector for Rita and suppressed his feelings. After the funeral he found himself spending more hours at work, actually dreading to come home. He knew his grief wasn't as intense as Rita's, that she had been with Judy more. But he began to lose patience when, after several months, Rita was still in deep self-blaming anguish.

Not until they contacted a SIDS organization did Rita hear other mothers express feelings akin to hers. She began to normalize her grief. Sam was supported by fathers who had dealt with their own guilt of not being able to fix things for their wives and families.

SUGGESTIONS FOR COPING AND HEALING

All of the forms of death in this chapter represent serious losses to the parents. The deaths that occur before birth cause the loss of the wishes and fantasies for the child and the loss of a future with that child. In terms of the parents' emotions, the baby was real and must be acknowledged. The parents' projections of that baby are stored in the unconscious. It is up to us to heal those memories and resolve the grief.

When the baby lives long enough to have formed solid attachments, grief is more intense. By now the child is known as a real person with a unique temperament and personality. The loss, especially if it is sudden, is overwhelming to the parents.

As a rule, the mother, because of her constant caregiving role, experiences the death with deeper grief than the father. It is typical in our culture for the father to act as the protector and the strong one for the family and to suppress his emotions. The parents' communication is an important element in keeping them close during this most difficult time.

Actions Immediately After the Loss

The paragraphs that follow offer suggestions for healing actions you can take immediately after the death of your child.

Prebirth Loss. Name your child so that he or she will have an identity. After a miscarriage one couple had a memorial christening with just one friend. They wrote their own funeral service to say goodbye to their unborn child. This helped the wife, in particular, to let go.

Loss of a Newborn. Insist on holding your baby if you are able. If it is physically impossible for the mother to attend the funeral or burial, plan a memorial service later. There needs to be closure, and closure is difficult when there has been no severance ritual.

If the nursery has been prepared before the birth, both parents should put things away together. It should be made clear that the husband's role is not to "fix it" but to join his wife in sharing grief openly.

Cremation is being used more often after newborns die. With cremation, the memorial service can be planned when the parents are ready. It is still important to initiate and carry through a ritual with the baby as the focus.

Loss in the Child's First or Second Year. Help dress your child if you possibly can. While everyone can't do it, those who did reported that helping with these preparations made all the difference in helping with their grief. One family brought their baby home from the funeral home in her casket, where she lay in state in the living room until the funeral. Because the parents couldn't sleep anyhow, sitting up with their child seemed an important thing that they could do for themselves and her.

Another couple, whose daughter died at home of a terminal illness, carried her themselves to the funeral home. They sat down with the funeral director to make the arrangements with their little girl still in the father's arms. The sensitive funeral director told the parents to stay there with her as long as they wanted. When they left, they said they were then ready to finally leave her.

The point of these stories is that time with the child after death is healing. Take the time you need to say good-bye, and make whatever gesture your heart prescribes.

Examples of Healing Responses

- Many couples write their children's funeral services. Such funerals are personalized and meaningful for the parents, family, and friends. Choosing music helps to access deep emotions. The funeral should be in a place where pain can be shared rather than held in.

- One couple carried their infant's casket in their car to the burial. The casket sat between them on the front seat, signifying to everyone that the child was still an important member of the family.

- An eight-year-old boy with a terminal illness wrote a poem before he died. The poem was read at the funeral.

- The day after her child died, a mother composed a song for the child and was able to sing it at the service.

Special Attention for Women Soon After Pregnancy

When death follows pregnancy, you have a special need to take care of yourself. The following list of suggestions will help you both psychologically and physically:

- Exercise—walking is a good outlet for your stored emotions and also an excellent way to improve cardiovascular functioning. Your body will heal faster, and you will sleep better.

- Maintain a well-balanced diet. Avoid alcohol or any other nonprescribed drugs. They usually increase depression rather than eliminate it.

- Make sure you get enough rest. Nap in the day if you can. If you are not sleeping well at night, use an audio tape that talks you through progressive muscle relaxation.

- Talk with others about any feelings. It is important to share your loss experience with another close friend. Relating the facts will make it more real. Sharing will also help you let go of your guilt and anger sooner.

- Recognize that you have a right to grieve. Give yourself time to do it no matter what others might say. You know your body best.

- Get rest. Your body is going through changes and will tire easily.

- Quick mood changes are normal. Don't be afraid of them.

- Allow others to help you. If they don't offer, take the matter into your own hands and ask for what you need. If you can't think of anything, make something up. You need the nurturance and attention now.

8

• • • • • • • • • • • •

The Importance of Mourning Rituals

THERE WAS another thing during the church that got me, and that was when they went to close the casket. This man was really . . . he didn't mean it personally . . . but he was very thoughtless when he flipped—and he did flip—the cover, you know the little thing that hangs all around the casket. He did flip it, and it covered part of her face. And that just, you know . . . it was so careless. I mean, he didn't take it slowly and tuck it in, he just went flip! and it was like, "Close the casket and let's get on to the cemetery."
—Bereaved mother, age 38

Having to hold funeral rituals for a child is almost beyond our comprehension. The fact that a child could die, could precede his or her parents, challenges our deepest belief system. One of the guiding myths in our society is that children should outlive their parents in order to perpetuate the family. When a child dies before his or her time, we feel robbed by our loss. They are too innocent to be swallowed up by death.

Moreover, funerals are grown-up events. They are, in many respects, celebrations of the person who has now gone. How can we celebrate a life that hasn't been completed? No matter what the age of the child, the parents of that child will always feel that their child's life ended before it had a chance to begin.

FUNERALS CAN BE FRIGHTENING

Funerals can frighten because they focus our attention on the mystery of death and on the myths surrounding it. Every culture has a death myth, a set of beliefs regarding the relationships between life and death. The predominant myth in our society is that death is the worst possible thing that can happen to us and so should be avoided at any cost.

Death is the end of life. The rituals of mourning force us to acknowledge the death and come to grips with our denial. We must finally admit to ourselves that the death has actually occurred.

FUNERALS ARE POWERFUL

Mourning rituals are powerful in that they give meaning and structure to our feelings. They provide the opportunity for us to outwardly express our sorrow in a socially approved atmosphere. Funerals bring support from others. We see that the community is standing with us, that we are not alone in our grief. Perhaps most important, funerals provide spiritual strength. Just at a time when we feel total despair, loss of control, and unprecedented emotional pain, the rituals of mourning supply the glue that holds us together through those awful first days. We are given the opportunity to openly turn to a Higher Power for strength and feel backed by our community. This not only validates us at a time when we feel weak, vulnerable, and insecure, but it validates the life of our child as well. Recognition is given to both the one who died and to the ones who must now begin their bereavement.

FUNERALS SUPPLY DIRECTION

Rituals not only supply strength, but they supply direction as well. When we involve ourselves, even in a small way, in the planning of the ritual and then carry through with the ritual itself, there is an unconscious force at work. Though we can't see it, feel it, or touch it, at some deep level we are aware that a change has been initiated, be it the separation of a person, or the acceptance of an event, or both. Through rituals, we involve ourselves in an ending and a beginning at the same time. We can look to mourning rituals to:

Tap a source of power and energy

Renew and regenerate our beliefs

Lend a sense of importance to our rite of passage

Put our beliefs into action

Give form to human life

Bring support from the community whether it is one or more people

Offer permission to grieve

When Jim died, I made all the classic errors possible regarding the funeral. Having had little exposure to death, my thought was to deny as much as possible and control everything I could. By moving through the rituals quickly, I felt we could get through our grief faster. I was wrong.

But I also have to remember that Jim died during the 1960s, when the philosophy of grief encouraged privacy in death-related matters. Would-be supporters felt bereaved parents would rather be alone, so they rationalized staying away by saying to themselves, "There are few words that can offer comfort, so it is best to stay away anyhow." Private funerals were not that unusual.

We had just moved to Florida before Jim's accident and hadn't established a circle of close friends. Looking back on it now, I see that we could have benefited by waiting several days for our friends and relatives to come from other places before we had the funeral. There was no need to hurry. The funeral director may or may not have presented me with that option—I don't recall. At any rate, Jim was killed on a Monday and we had a small family funeral 1½ days later. By Wednesday evening all the rituals were over, everyone gone. What a sad little empty family we were.

There are few, if any, cultures other than our own in which mourning rituals are all over within days of the death. Traditional societies all recognize that the process of mourning requires months and years. Many other cultures provide rituals that facilitate mourning at several points across time. In our culture, many are beginning to question our customary use of the funerary and burial rites as the only rituals offered.

As important as funerals are in offering spiritual strength and direction, they are over just when our grief is beginning. There is nothing in between the beginning and the end of grief to mark the various changes which are subtly occurring. We cannot go back to widow's weeds, but we must find psychologically and spiritually satisfying new alternatives.

As I said earlier, the mourning rituals—the visitation, the wake, the funeral or memorial service, and the burial service—offer us an important connection through the first days after our loss. They are like punctuation points moving us relentlessly on from time to time, place to place, providing direction and guidance at a time we feel desperately lost.

Since the beginning of man, rituals have been an integral element of life. It is not possible to separate the process of mythologizing from the process of ritualizing. Our cultural myths represent our deepest beliefs. When we validate those traditional assumptions by acting out rituals, a life-sustaining power can ease us through the uncertainty surrounding the radical change. When I speak of myths, I am not talking about mere fantasy. Myth is, instead, the deep belief system, the world view, that shapes the structure of any culture. Myth gives order to sensory experience and fills the basic need for meaning in life. Behavior is to rituals what belief is to myths. Our rituals make our myths incarnate through our ritual behaviors.

The vast social changes in the past one hundred years in America have scattered the population, separating families from each other. It used to be that folks gew up, lived, and died within a small radius. When community members went through a death, family, friends, and relatives were nearby to support and help. People didn't feel isolated, and the traditions of the society were carried on quite naturally. Everyone knew what those traditions were and how to participate.

At that time, death came more frequently, particularly to children. Not that the frequency of loss made it any easier to bear; I'm sure the death of a child has always generated deep sorrow. But families were larger then. It was not unusual for a couple to have a dozen children before the mother was thirty-five and for the couple to lose two or three in birth or infancy. My grandmother had eleven children and died in the birth of the last one. That same winter a flu epidemic took the lives of two other of her children. My grandfather had to manage the family alone. The shock of the tragedy was somewhat lessened by the knowledge and expectation that these situations did happen and happened often. More children died than old people.

When Jim was killed suddenly that Labor Day afternoon, it was as if the shock of the event created a screen around me that blocked out the horrible reality. I remember coming home from the hospital after we had been told he was dead and facing my mother and little Catherine. I didn't have to say anything, I guess. They knew what had happened from my expression, although I couldn't cry. I felt as if I was watching myself go through the motions; I didn't feel like me. The sky overhead was black with a coming storm—storms happen suddenly in Florida. Years later, when the sky got this dark again, Catherine said to me, "Someone must have gotten killed just now." I didn't realize anyone had noticed the sky that day except me. I was a world apart.

I went through Jim's funerary rituals in the same manner, like a ghost. We went to the funeral home, but I couldn't face going into the selection room to choose a casket. I felt frozen, moving only when I had to. Very little was recorded in my conscious mind during that time. People came, people left. I'm sure I spoke to them, but I have no concrete memory of doing so. Events seemed to blur one into another as my mind reeled with the impossible realization that Jim was gone. Nothing made sense. I trudged leadenly through those awful ritual days before my grief really began.

THE FINAL RITES OF PASSAGE

Traditional cultures had some form of permission built into the ritual repertoire. For example, at a certain age approval was given to the young man or woman who desired to become an adult. There was a ritual of passage to mark that transition. The ritual itself contained implicit understanding of the changes being made.

In our culture today, in contrast, rituals have diminished. Families live far apart and communities are strangers to themselves. Exceptional transitions in our lives are handled on our own, as best we can without guidelines, community backing, sanctions, or permissions. Yet, through meaningful rituals, we desperately need to give expression to our transitions.

The Need for Rituals

When a child dies, we usually have little experience on which to base our needs. We are thrown into a state of shock and disbelief. The thought of having to make "arrangements" causes us to recoil in horror. Just at the time we are expected to make important decisions, we are agonizing over our own loss and blindly groping for any possibility that would tell us it isn't real. Jenny, a young bereaved mother, shared her story with me about her daughter's funeral:

> I had to be told several times before anything would register. I'm screaming to myself, No, no, it isn't true, and someone is asking me what Missy should wear. What to wear, my God . . . I wanted her back—back in her little overalls, playing in the yard. What happened? Why? These questions kept me so occupied. Yet, in spite of my mind racing, we had to make decisions, God forbid, about her funeral.

Jenny said she didn't even know what she was doing during those first few days. It was over before she came out of "the fog," as she described it. Too quickly the rituals were over, family had returned to their homes in other towns, and Jenny was expected to grieve a little while and then return to her job.

I couldn't do it. I couldn't go back to the office that soon. A lot of good I would do anyhow—probably cry all the time. I didn't know what I was supposed to do, you know. There was nowhere to go or nothing to be. Everything had changed, but everyone acted like nothing had.

Jenny and I talked about the possibility of building more rituals into her bereavement so that she would have points along the way that would somehow connect her, points of transition. She could continue these rituals until her grief had reached the renewal phase. The forward motion of the sequential rituals would build hope into her life—hope that the intense suffering she was living with now would someday end.

Three Parts of All Rites of Passage

Three steps emerge over and over in all rites of passage, and ancient primitive societies devised elaborate rituals around each of these parts. Whether the ritual was to commemorate a marriage or a death, these three steps appeared:

Severance—that part of the ritual that represents separation—an ending.

Transition—that phase that represents the gradual change from one state to another.

Reincorporation—the acknowledgment of a re-entry into a new life, a new beginning.

Our final rite of passage usually comes after many other passages throughout our life. Some of the passages include baptism, puberty, leaving home, marriage, having children, divorce, midlife crisis, dealing with an "empty nest," retirement or major career shift, illness, and death. All these events are life passages and need some form of ritual to help us move through the difficult transitions that each one produces.

Our society offers little with which to bridge the empty months and even years of grief after a death. It ignores the end of grief, the reincorporation, and leaves the bereaved hanging—with no community support and few with whom to share. In the Jewish faith, in contrast, bereavement begins with a week of shiva. This is where the family sits together to share sorrow for seven days. Family members are excused from work and given this special time to deal with their shock and loss. Then, each week of the first month and every month during the first year, the loss is acknowledged in the synagogue. At the year's end, a celebration of reincorporation welcomes the bereaved back into the mainstream of the community. Even when grief is far from over at this time, the celebration is a vote of confidence from the community, an acknowledgment that grievers have survived terrible upheaval.

SELF-MADE MOURNING RITUALS

To supplement our current mourning rituals, it is my belief that we could benefit tremendously by participating in smaller community-supported rituals. Gather a small number of people you trust together and decide what would be supportive—what rituals would give meaning to the passage and at the same time build in the expectation for the eventual easing of the suffering. Participants must keep in mind that the death of a child takes much longer to process than any other single bereavement. Even when the intense agony of grief is past, there will always be special anniversaries, birthdays, and holidays to contend with. Knowing that there will be a special tribute, a group to count on, a ritual to perform that will carry you through, reduces the fear. We are sustained by the acknowledgment given to our beloved children on their special days.

In this regard I do want to mention The Compassionate Friends, an organization active throughout the country in helping bereaved parents and family members who have experienced the death of a child. If there isn't a chapter near you, write to the national headquarters in Illinois; I have included the address and phone number in Chapter 14. The staff will be able to help you start a chapter in your area.

There are some people, however, who don't do well in groups. They are private in grief and prefer to be with only one or two trusted friends. If you feel this way, don't let this stop you from benefiting from appropriate rituals. You will gain strength both emotionally and intellectually when you can draw upon the spiritual power available to you. Finding meaning in life again and sharing the process with others can begin to unite you once again with your community and build trust in the world.

Planning Self-Made Rituals

Bereavements contain anniversaries and specific periods that are extremely painful. You approach each date with dread and are fearful that you won't be able to get through the day. Confront that fear by actually planning the day and incorporating a small ritual of your own. Suppose you dread the birthday of your deceased child, for example. You might arrange an activity that acknowledges the birthday—you could look at photographs of a past birthday celebration or light the number of candles that would represent the age of your child this year. To share this ritual with the family or a few friends, you could ask each to read something that reminds them of your child and then light one of the candles to represent the spiritual connection among you and to your child. The tools you use in your ritual or when or how you do it don't matter; the important aspect is thoughtful planning. A ritual planned ahead of time directs attention toward the expectations for a positive outcome.

Tools for Ritual Builders: Symbols

We have any number of useful tools at our disposal when we begin to plan a ritual The list that follows presents a few of them to give you an idea of the array:

- Music—Melodies and rhythm speak directly to the intuitive level of awareness. They evoke a deep emotional response and move us at the deepest level of the unconscious. Music could be a tape of your child's favorite song or one where words are meaningful.

- Invocation—Self-generated rituals often include some form of calling on a source of energy, such as a Higher Power or some other divine force, to be present with the participants. An invocation focuses the awareness of the participants on the memorialized child and also on a common source of power.

- Silence—Participants can often employ silence as a method of tuning in to each other in a particularly meaningful way. Silence may involve meditation or contemplation and is often used as an opening to the ritual experience.

- Vows—Rituals often include vows, which can be powerful psychological reinforcements of personal commitment to change. By verbalizing the desired outcome, the expectation for change is put into motion. A vow can be used to strengthen the belief that the child is being taken care of by a Higher Power or that pain and suffering can eventually be left behind us.

- Incense and smoke—These ascending symbols have long been viewed as a way to make contact with the world of the spirit. Smoke is symbolic of transcendence and purification.

- Feasting—The sharing of food and drink is a universal symbol of agreement or mutual commitment. It is used traditionally at the end of all rituals to indicate the joining of the community in love and support.

Rena, the bereaved mother of Tammy, used many symbols in the ritual she planned to commemorate Tammy's sixth birthday, ten months after the child's death. Rena knew it was going to be an awful day. She knew she would not be able to forget Tammy's fifth birthday party, her last, and her excited little face as she greeted each small guest. Tammy was like that, her mother said. She always entered into things with so much enthusiasm. That was the birthday Tammy got her new bike—a wave of nausea rolls over Rena every time she remembers giving the bike to Tammy. Two months later, the bike caused Tammy's death.

The grief had been hell for Rena. She dreaded Tammy's birthday, thinking, "I can't get through it. I'll go crazy, I know." An article on the power of self-generated rituals had given her the idea of using a ritual to help her through the grievous day. As Rena began to plan the ritual, she could feel a sense of sustaining strength move through her.

Rena invited her four closest friends to come at 11:00, an hour before she planned to serve lunch. Rena asked them to write a brief statement of how they remembered Tammy and what she had meant to them. Rena took care of the other plans.

Before her friends arrived, Rena put a portrait of Tammy on a living room table with some fresh spring flowers to represent the child's innocent beauty and radiance. A lighted candle represented the spiritual connection.

When her friends gathered in the living room, Rena was already in tears but vowed she would continue in the hope that the ritual would be less difficult. Everyone knew why they were there, and so the focus remained on Tammy.

Rena began with a silent meditation to draw them together in a common experience. She then played a tape of gentle music, one that she used to play when Tammy was going to sleep. While the music played softly, Rena read a group of poems that had been favorites of Tammy's. Rena told me that all her friends were crying with her, but that their shared grief encouraged her to go on. She began to feel a little stronger.

After that, Rena asked each one to read what they had written for Tammy. One friend read a beautiful poem describing Tammy's growth from infancy on. This part ended with Rena sharing some of her thoughts about how Tammy was cared for now and what she was doing in her afterlife. This part lifted them up a little and depicted Tammy as the wonderfully alive little person she had been and would always be in their hearts.

Rena put on a happier tape that Tammy had liked to tap dance to (as she called it). As it was playing, Rena reversed the order of lunch and brought in a birthday cake with six candles on it. She asked each friend to light a candle in positive remembrance of Tammy.

Rena shared with me later that she was worried that her friends would think she was crazy. Actually, it was just the opposite. They all agreed that they should repeat the ritual next year. It had not only helped them all deal with the death, but it had brought them all together in a peak experience, creating closeness and love.

The Power of Self-Made Rituals

Though funerals and memorial services will always be the initial rites of passage following a death, the power of self-generated rituals can carry us through the following months and years of bereavement. We become involved in the rituals we create, and the power of the personal ritual arises from both creating it and carrying it out. When, like Rena, we invest ourselves in the planning and development of the particular ritual, we tap a sustaining source of power and hope.

Rena learned another important fact about self-made rituals: When we bond together in symbolic reality, we bring others into our lives, our crises, and also into our healthy renewal. We connect in a deep intuitive way.

Rituals require us to surrender ourselves to the process that we have set into motion. Rena learned that once she gave herself to the ritual, became vulnerable to it, her trust that grief would some day end was strengthened.

Rituals don't have to be elaborate. They should, however, incorporate one or more of the tools mentioned earlier. And, to repeat, preplanning is necessary for the ritual to carry the unified focus we wish to commemorate.

When we give importance to the painful events as well as to their release or pleasurable happenings, we give full expression to our lives. We create peak experiences. We transcend the bleak, dark times and uphold the spiritual, light moments. While we pray that we won't ever have to go through another loss of a child, we know that there will be other painful situations where we must say goodbye forever to one we dearly love. Facing the realities with meaningful rituals shared with trusted friends can give us courage and strength to confront our next difficult loss.

One couple had the graveside service for their son first, with close family members, and then attended an open memorial service. The mother explained that she didn't want the rituals to end on the down tone she felt the burial would create. Supporters at the memorial service were asked to share what the ten-year-old had meant to them, how his life had touched them. After eight to ten people had spoken, a small girl stood and said, "He meant a lot to me 'cause I just loved him."

We have an enormous need to move away from stiff, formal liturgies and return to more meaningful, personalized, and spiritually uplifting rituals. Funeral directors should be willing and ready to help with whatever type of service you need.

When a child dies, the shock immobilizes you so completely that you may need to leave the first funerary services to others who don't know your child. Do what you can to participate, however; your participation will help you heal. For example, provide as much information as you can to the person who will conduct the service. Allow him or her to know about your family and your child so the service will reflect you. As shock recedes, remember that you can devise your own meaningful rituals whenever you are ready—and that you can repeat or continue to create rituals as long as you need to.

Your life will be strengthened and supported by the meaning you put into your rites of passage, and you will gain spiritual courage through the connection you make with yourself, your family, and your friends.

9

· · · · · · · · · · · · ·

Surviving the Emptiness

Not a day goes by that I don't think of Timmy. But it's different now. Before, I used to remember the hospital—seeing him all hooked up to tubes and wires and all that. I kept seeing his frail little body . . . and how scared I was. . . . Those kinds of memories would haunt me every day. But now, it's been four years. That may seem like a long time—it is a long time. But now, I see Timmy in a different way. I see him before he got sick, happy all the time. I remember the good times we had together and for the first time since he died, I can look at pictures without them choking me up.

—Bereaved father, age 33

When your child dies a large part of you is gone forever too. The wound cuts deeply, the scar tissue is slow to heal. You aren't even sure you want the wound to heal. That wound may be your only connection to your lost child. Yet the wound is hard to bear, and you are pulled irrevocably toward a quieter place in grief—a place deep within where you might find peace.

The first two phases of grief are filled with turmoil. You blindly grope your way through each day, grasping at anything that might bring your child back. Bargaining is a part of the intense yearning. If you wish hard enough, yearn deeply enough, then perhaps you'll get your child back. Your focus is directed toward regaining your child through your pain.

After Jim was killed, I remember feeling that I was being buffeted by an angry storm. I felt fatigued, frustrated, hopelessly trapped in a no-win situation. The pain was incredible, but there was no way to make it stop. I wanted to go to sleep like Rip van Winkle and wake up twenty years later. Or not wake up at all. Anything to rid myself of the insufferable yearning.

Fears mounted. My motivation to cling to anything stable became almost an obsession. I was to learn later that there wasn't anything stable outside myself.

THE NEED TO SURRENDER

Fear during the first months following the death of a child is a natural response for most of us. We fear something happening to our other children, or our spouses, or ourselves. The shock we experienced lives on in our bodies, and we are reminded over and over of its killing effect as we continue to uncover new ungrieved areas. We access new grief by finding an old favorite toy while cleaning out the garage, uncovering the child's ski mask with the winter things, or seeing the lost child's best friend now skipping off with another best friend. Small things, but devastating. Life continues on—but without us.

Yet the body has a way of deciding what to do. After the exhaustion of the first two phases of grief, the body provides clear indicators of the need to withdraw and conserve what energy is left. We begin to sleep more. When we have been sleeping poorly for months, this change makes us uneasy. Is this a clinical depression? We are confused by the fatigue. Whereas the first two phases were marked by restlessness, we now sit and stare—at nothing. We have moved into another phase of grief, which is marked by the need to rest and restore depleted physical and emotional resources.

This is a time-out period, one that offers an opportunity to move inward into ourselves. The period can be frightening because the distractions we used in the first phases of grief—anger, guilt, weeping, and screaming— no longer have the same cathartic effect.

Out of necessity, phase 3 becomes a period of surrender. Surrender to the tragic realization that the child won't return ever. Surrender to the awful emptiness and to the struggle we made against it. Surrender to the despair. We have to stop and go within ourselves.

This was especially hard for Joan to do because, all her life, she had been active and busy. When their daughter, Marcy, died at only eighteen, Joan tried to continue her life as she had always done. Marcy had been born with cystic fibrosis and had required a lot of attention during her lifetime. So much had been required of Joan and her husband Richard in caring for Marcy, but they wouldn't have ever traded a single moment of being with her. They truly adored their daughter. Because Joan and Richard had expected her death on many other occasions, they had had ample opportunity to arrange everything ahead of time. They felt that they had even grieved ahead of time.

The funeral arrangements, like other preparations, had been made well in advance. Each member of the family participated in the service, reading a special poem or prose they had written. People told them it was one of the most moving services they had ever attended—that it was uplifting and lovingly spiritual.

Joan and Richard were deeply grieved but felt satisfied that everything possible had been done for Marcy. She had lived long past the time that she was expected to, and they were happy with that.

Joan continued her busy life, taking care of the home, making the other girls' clothes, doing church work, participating in several organizations. Maybe even busier than before, she said, because now she had even more time to give. They all missed Marcy terribly, but their routines hadn't changed. Joan felt glad that she hadn't been overcome with grief and attributed this to the anticipatory grieving she had done before Marcy died.

Around nine months after the death, Joan came down with a serious case of flu. She needed to be in bed but was up and down during the day anyhow. She felt exhausted, but it was difficult for her to stay still for very long. Her mind would race from one thing to another.

Recovery was slow. Just when she felt a little better, she would slide back into another bout. Joan would try to get some enthusiasm for the day, but in only a little while she would fall back into bed or collapse on the couch.

After a complete physical checkup, the doctor explained her situation: "You're completely exhausted—what we call battle fatigue. Apparently, Marcy's death was a greater shock than you realized. You have been using all your energy trying to deny your grief and at the same time keeping a backbreaking schedule."

Joan interrupted: "But I have had loads of energy all along."

"It may have seemed like you had a lot of energy," the

doctor retorted, "but what was happening was that you were burning your own high-powered drug, adrenaline. It kept you going, but it also weakened your immune system. Your body called a halt and put you in bed with the flu. Our bodies have a way of taking over when there is a need. You just didn't hear it earlier because you were so into your denial."

Knowing what would happen if she went home, he insisted that she go to the hospital for a week of complete bed rest. He also suggested that he call in a counselor specializing in grief. Joan agreed. She knew she was very tired and at last seemed willing to have others take over.

This was the point at which Joan began to surrender. Her life wasn't working. No matter how much she did, there was a deep core of sadness that she couldn't obliterate. She was ready for a time-out period, she said.

TIME-OUT

A time-out period is not useless time. Time-out allows us to have a better perspective on the life journey we are making. If we move too quickly, we would continue in the haze that we experienced during the shock phase; we would always be riding the roller coaster without a glimmer of what was going on. Fortunately, this period of quiet is exactly what we need to assimilate life slowly, so that we can be ready for the new way of living that is to come.

When we lose a significant person through death, our lives are never the same again. We are changed through the long process of bereavement. There has been an ending—an ending we don't want to acknowledge. Eventually, however, the truth becomes evident, and we must adjust to a different world without the dearly loved person. When that person is a child, finding our way toward inner peace seems especially long and tedious. Sometimes we despair of ever finding our way.

I used to wonder why grief took so long. Why couldn't we grieve for maybe a year and then not hurt so much? Why did we resist resolution so vehemently? Especially when resolution could lead us to peace and serenity.

After Jim died, I seemed to stay in the conservation/ withdrawal phase of grief for a long time. I wondered if that was the way I would always be. Maybe I wasn't doing grief right. What was wrong with me that I couldn't get over it? Others did it. I almost drove myself crazy thinking that I was going crazy.

Since then, I have come to know that most bereaved people feel that way at one time or another—that they are going a little crazy. I have also come to realize that it takes a long time to move from one reality to another. If we try to do it too quickly, we end up nowhere—having lost the past, but not searched long enough to find the new person within us or the new beginning. The rites of passage in most traditional societies allowed adequate time to make the slow connection between the old and the new. We don't have any such rites to live by today. We must allow ourselves an adequate time-out period in which to process and allow changes to take place gradually.

Taking a time-out doesn't mean that you shut down your life. When you feel exhausted and run down, unable to cope with everyday problems, seek some quiet time for yourself. Choose a time and place where no one is making demands on you and where you can isolate yourself from your own undue demands. Take a weekend alone at the beach, for example, or the mountains— whichever place brings more peace. During that time look at your life, comprehend the ending that has taken place, and prepare yourself for the transition that is beginning. You'll know when it is the right time to give up the pain; you'll feel the gentle tug offered by your Higher Power. You'll be ready to give up the pain eventually.

Joan learned that the first requirement for time-out is to let go, surrender, give in to the emptiness and stop struggling against it. If we use so much energy pushing against pain, trying to keep it from getting too near, we have very little strength left to resolve grief or deal with the inevitable changes that are taking place as a result of the loss.

It seems paradoxical that, to resolve pain, we have to face it and walk directly into it. Grief work requires that of us. No matter how busy we are or how much we deny, once we slow our thoughts down, we always come back to the same ruminations of the lost child. In these ruminations, in going over and over the life shared with the child, we finally loosen our grip on the illusion—the illusion that the child will return. We then slowly face the cold reality: The old conditions are gone. Life will never be the same again.

Only then do we really begin to accept the loss, realizing that changes will have to take place in all phases of life. In doing this we do begin to see that grief is a death and resurrection experience. We must die to the old life while at the same time watching a new one slowly form.

I'm not sure that a resurrection can ever be fully accomplished without the help of some guiding and sustaining force—a power greater than ourselves. We can come just so far on our own. Clare learned this as she tried to survive her son's accidental death.

Clare, a thirty-nine-year-old single parent, had been divorced for four years. Her son Tommy was eleven; her daughter Gwen was seven. Both children were legally in Clare's custody because her ex-husband had left one day, saying he could no longer take the responsibility of a family. What Clare learned later was that he had met someone new and wanted to be with her. He was transferred to another state shortly after that. Clare lost track of him. An independent person, she managed to take care of the children by totally devoting her life to it.

Clare always called the house when it was time for Tommy to get home from school. He was a good student, completing his homework as soon as he got home. Gwen stayed at a neighbor's house until Tommy went to get her. One day Clare called Tommy from work and there was no answer. She called a half hour later. No answer. Nothing 30 minutes after that. Now she was worried. Since it was close to 5:30, her usual quitting time, she rushed home.

When she turned into her street, she saw a crowd gathered on the front lawn three doors down from her house. That's where Allen lived, Tommy's best friend. Clare could see an ambulance and two police cars. Her mind began to race. Had something happened to Allen or Allen's mother? She rushed into her house, calling to Tommy, then to Gwen. No one was home. Must be down at Allen's, with the crowd. Clare ran across the lawns, heart racing, near panic. Just then the ambulance driver came out of the house with a stretcher—covered.

At that moment, she saw Allen's mother inside the house. Rushing in, she asked, "What happened? Who was hurt?" When Allen's mother saw Clare, she burst into tears and covered her face. She mumbled something about Clare never forgiving them.

Clare's legs were growing weak. She could barely stand up. "Where is Tommy? Is anything wrong with Tommy?" Allen's mother sobbed out her horrible answer: "Tommy's been shot. Allen was showing him Ken's gun, and it went off. Clare, Tommy's dead. I'm so sorry. I'm so sorry," she kept repeating. The ambulance's sirens wailed their awful sound as it drove off. Clare fainted.

Grief for Clare was an unending torment. Her life had focused on Tommy. Since the divorce he had been her best friend, a surrogate husband. The emptiness was unbearable. She tried groups. She tried individual thera-

py. Her emotions vacillated between guilt for leaving
Tommy alone and anger at him for going to Allen's house
before his homework was finished. Shame mounted; she
could almost hear others talking about how she left her
children alone.

Gwen felt the loneliness too, because Tommy had been
such a good big brother. Fortunately, Clare found a play
therapy group for her where she was helped with her
feelings of loss.

Three years went by, and for Clare the sadness seemed
to be as painful as it had been earlier. Clare was too
angry at God to even think of letting go. It was as if she
needed to hang on to her resentments for Tommy to be
mourned properly.

But she was tired and she knew it. Gwen loved the
beach and begged her mother to take her there on their
vacation. Clare heard about Sanibel Island—not too big
a crowd, lots of shells. She found a beachfront condo-
minium there and booked it for two weeks.

Sanibel turned out to be the perfect choice. As she
began to relax, gain perspective on her life, and face the
reality of her loss, she slowly loosened her grip on her
anger. Walking the beach alone, early in the morning
while Gwen watched TV, she started talking to Tommy.
She told him how much she missed him, how she wished
he could be back. She described the sunrises, the way
the sun glistened on the waves, various shells she found.
Clare had given up on the "whys" now, because she knew
there were no answers.

One day, during her early-morning walk, she asked
Tommy what she should do about her life. A voice in her
heart said, "Move on." She was startled by the strength of
that answer, but she took it seriously. As she reflected on
it, she began to see that she had put life on hold for too
long. She had not grown. In terms of her own development and her connections with others, she had even lost
ground.

Clare realized that she had locked herself in with

only a few friends for several years, even before Tommy had died. She had used the excuse that she was too busy to expand her circle, but now she could see that she had limited herself as a protection. She had been hurt when her husband had left, and she didn't want to be hurt like that again so she had withdrawn from life somewhat. Then, when Tommy was killed, she closed up entirely. To move on, she realized, she was going to have to let people in.

When she heard the "voice" on the beach, she had no doubt that it was real. Whether it was Tommy or some divinely inspired guidance, she trusted that it held meaning for her. This was Clare's turning point. She had experienced her resurrection. Tommy was no longer completely absent; he had assumed a new place in her life. Part of her task now was to find not only new directions for herself, but also what her new relationship with Tommy meant. She had to let him go emotionally, she knew that, but now some of the enormous heaviness had lifted.

She couldn't wait to share this with Gwen. Her daughter represented another area where she had shut down. She and Gwen rarely talked of Tommy, but in their thoughts he was always there like a great boulder between them. Suddenly, she could see how keeping Tommy alive in a healthy way through shared memories could enhance both their lives.

When we have come through a transcending experience like Clare's, we often worry that the effect won't last—that we might fall back into the way we have been suffering. That's why we need to be alert to small (or large) sources of energy. The source could be any change—a vacation that offers a new perspective, taking a course, a new job, starting volunteer work—and the effect could be an experience like Clare's, or something quite different. When we find ourselves opening to change, we are seeing a sign of the beginning of a healing process that eventually frees us from the insufferable pain and yearning.

The death of a child is like an amputation. It is a severing of a bond that is like an extension of the parent's physical body. The loss seems so palpable that the bereaved often seek medical attention for a particular physical symptom. Healing only comes, however, by changing internal concepts. Each parent must give up the concept of "my child" and learn to live independently with oneself. As such, bereavement is a time of change, of transcending one phase to achieve another. Bereavement is most definitely a death and resurrection experience.

In his book *Transitions,* William Bridges tells us that all transitions begin with endings. Endings are followed by a period of confusion and conflict, but they finally lead to the possibility of new beginnings. I stress the word "possibility," because we do have a choice. We can choose to remain stuck in our resistance to change, blocking the hope for renewal, or we can, instead, choose the opportunity to move forward. This takes courage and persistence. But when we have already come through the worst thing that could happen to us, what worse thing can we fear?

When we lose a child or any significant loved one, who we used to be has changed. The people we are capable of becoming must be resurrected in new form. This takes time, but it is well worth the effort. Life is full of risks, but until we accept them we will never be able to move beyond that place of hurting.

In the beginning of grief, the thought of giving up pain isn't to be considered. After all, if our precious child is dead, what right do we have to benefit from being alive? The idea of growth is unthinkable then. As we suffer through bereavement, however, we undergo a gradual change. There is no way to avoid it. Everything in life has changed already just because of the fact that our child is no longer here. The world seems empty, as do our lives and our bodies. We begin to react to the changes whether we want to or not. If we merely react to the outer changes, we will simply be adjusting our old selves to fit the new circumstances and pain will continue. To be resurrected, we need to incorporate inner changes. The inner changes that are needed will be made evident by listening to the guidance of inner urgings, of trusting that guidance and being willing to take small steps toward developing our potential. To hear the guidance, we must learn to center ourselves.

DEVELOPING THE POWER WITHIN: CENTERING

A major step in rebuilding is learning to center ourselves. Centering is the process of coming to know the essential self, of becoming aware of what we need for ourselves. The true core provides a solid base from which to work out crises and problems. Only in knowing who we are can we know what we need in life. Joan told me that all her life she had lived as others had wanted her to live, her husband included. She said she hadn't known the difference between her happiness and theirs—that, to her, happiness lay in making others happy. If they weren't happy, she couldn't be happy. She hadn't a clue about how to make herself content. When her daughter Marcy died, Joan was at a total loss as to what to do with her life. She stayed busy because she was afraid her life was over. But gradually she learned, after she began to center herself, that she could let go of trying to be what someone else wanted. She could actually claim some happiness for herself, simply by fulfilling some inner longings of her own. It was a revelation to her, she said. But it also meant hard practice on her part. Letting go

of her constant focus on others' needs and learning
what it meant to be at home with herself required great
effort initially. Later, she was able to recognize her own
feelings, not someone else's. She developed a new sense
of trust in herself. Joan said:

> I always felt that loving God was being responsible for
> others, and so I tried to do all that I could to make
> others happy. But what I didn't realize was that, in
> doing that, I was ignoring God in me. I learned that
> what I really wanted was the thanks of others. When
> I didn't get thanks in return for something I had done,
> I felt deflated, discounted. It's different now. I still do
> for others, but I do it out of my fullness rather than
> my emptiness.

For Joan, doing for others was a way of keeping control. When she began to center herself, her life became
more fulfilled than she could ever have believed possible.
She began to live out of a true sense of love for herself.

Several methods are useful in centering ourselves:
meditation, psychotherapy, and deep relaxation are a few.
Anything that can be used to quiet your mind and allow
self-awareness to move from the outside to the inside will
work.

Meditation

This is the best method I know for getting in touch with
the inner self. Nevertheless, our society has a difficult
time understanding the process of meditation. Because
we are oriented toward activity, most of us find it hard
to sit quietly and simply feel or listen. The work ethic
fills us with the notion that, unless we are actively
pursuing a valid goal, we are wasting time. As a result,
we have come to value the world around us and neglect

the world within. Meditation allows us the opportunity to reconnect with our deeper values.

Meditation is an effective way to quiet the mind and access the unconscious. The unconscious is where we store all our learning, thoughts, and feelings. These unconscious reserves are the basis of spiritual wisdom, which every individual possesses, though not everyone is aware of possessing it. Our greatest creativity is unleashed when we tap that unconscious wisdom. Only until we are able to find our way into the unconscious do we open the possibilities of solving our life dilemmas, of understanding our deepest desires, and of discovering directions we long for.

Some methods of meditation utilize chanting, ritual prayer, or visualization. Most community colleges and churches offer classes to teach you how to meditate. A phone call or two will certainly locate some help for you. The important point is to get started and learn the process of turning inward for spiritual strength and guidance.

Psychotherapy

Getting to know ourselves better is a worthy goal when making a new transition in life. Many of the coping mechanisms we use habitually are outworn and outdated. Processing thoughts, feelings, and behaviors with a therapist can open the way to letting go of old dysfunctional mechanisms because psychotherapy offers constant feedback.

Psychotherapy is also a time to discover what we really want out of life. It sometimes is a trial-and-error situation, but if you keep at it and don't worry about mistakes, you will gain both practice and confidence. Your experiences become an important means of knowing yourself and where you want to go with your life.

Deep Relaxation

Relaxation allows the body to release neuromuscular hypertension, which keeps you uptight and anxious. Like meditation, relaxation opens the unconscious and lets you reach your inner wisdom. When used regularly, deep relaxation allows greater restfulness, calmness, and general feelings of well-being. One way to achieve deep relaxation is to listen to one of the many relaxation audiotapes that are commercially available. By offering music and words that have a calming influence, these tapes can help the listener relax his or her entire body.

Other Suggestions for Centering

Nena and George O'Neil, in their important book *Shifting Gears,* list several techniques that can help you make use of your time-out periods and discover your true center.

- Don't be afraid to waste time—The O'Neils advocate the enjoyment of unstructured moments throughout the day. In our uptight society of worry and compulsive behavior, we lose perspective. We feel that if we don't have a purpose for everything we do, we aren't pulling our load.

    That's nonsense!

    Your most important responsibility in life is to develop yourself to your fullest potential. If you spend all your time distracting yourself from that task, you remain in a cul-de-sac. Your most creative times come from those wonderful lazy moments when you let go of the pressures around you. I call these moments hammock times.

- Daydream—The O'Neils call daydreaming a time of mental drifting and wandering. Being open to your daydreams can open you to your intuitive self so you can get in touch with your needs, desires, and hopes. This is a big step toward changing your life by drawing upon your valuable inner resources.

• Check things out with yourself—Get rid of the "shoulds" and "oughts" in your life. For instance, instead of saying "I have to . . ." say "I choose to. . . ." Or change "I can't . . ." to "I'd rather not. . . ." Each of these examples means a change of attitude and habit.

• Don't be afraid to say no—Saying no is an important way to prevent people from owning you. When you are afraid to say no, you sell out to what other people want you to be. The inability to say no is the cornerstone of all addictions. Developing the healthy ability to say no to those things that you find neither interesting nor healthy can release you to other, happier alternatives. Saying yes may seem like the easiest way out, but if you really don't want to do something and then force yourself to do it, you lose your personal power. Rather than feeling centered, you feel more scattered.

• Discover your feelings by talking about them—This is where a good friend, someone who will listen without judging and someone you trust, comes into play. Brainstorming with another, sifting through your feelings, you begin to find which feelings are real or useful. When you can pull up elements of hidden guilt or shame, you then have the opportunity to truly let those feelings go. Most of the guilt you burden yourself with is nurtured by keeping your feelings tightly locked up. By taking the lid off, you clear out old guilts and shameful thoughts. Once out, they are never as bad as we thought they were.

The O'Neils' suggestions are excellent; any one of them would make a good starting point for a time-out period. Taking a journey into emptiness is an opportunity to divest yourself of the grief you carry. "Tapes" of old criticisms, corrections, "ought to's," and "shoulds" can be eliminated. Once you have let go of these outdated demands you make on yourself, you are free to employ new useful tapes you create to help yourself rather than make yourself afraid. But you must be willing to face the emptiness to make self-discoveries.

When you take the time to truly know yourself, you not only find new directions in life, but you can also learn to have greater confidence in yourself. Once you have found your center and begin to live by the needs and desires that truly belong to you, you can maintain an easy balance in life. You become less dependent and more capable of intimacy with others.

SEARCHING FOR MEANING IN LIFE

When a child has died, the question of meaning is always there in the back of our minds. The constant "Why?" in the beginning is part of this. We are plagued by the need to find any answer that could explain this enormous mystery. Each parent asks "How could God allow my child to die and leave me here? What good am I? What is the meaning of life now that everything has changed?" These questions cannot be answered easily or quickly.

Not until we have gained some distance from the shock of loss, worked through the realization and acknowledgment of the death, and begun to accept the inevitable changes occurring can we start to answer questions concerning the meaning of life. As we gain spiritual strength from centering ourselves, we will also gain guidance in the directions to take. Then, as these directions begin to lead us to places where we can find satisfactions while renewing our confidence, we find our faith in the world slowly returning.

Grief is a long arduous process, painful beyond belief. Don't feel you must rush it or be disappointed if you don't move as fast as you think you "should." There is no right or wrong way to grieve, just your way. You are entitled to as much time as you need. You are also entitled to your own mistakes. Without mistakes, I can guarantee there haven't been enough risks. And without risks, there is no growth.

Your courage and perseverance have gotten you to this point in your grief—a point of new beginnings. The scar tissue is healing, and the severe pain has lessened tremendously. What grief has taught you is waiting to be practiced.

10

· · · · · · · · · · ·

Beginning to
Live Once More

I KNEW grief was going to be long and terrible, so I gave myself time and space to deal with it . . . and it was just as long and terrible as I thought. But I figured some day it would be over and I'd be able to move on with my life— sadly, without Bobby, I knew that. Our family would be smaller and we'd always miss him. But what I hadn't figured on was that I was changing all the time I was grieving. I didn't realize that part. And when I came out the other side, I hardly knew myself. I had changed, and I didn't even know it.

—Bereaved mother, age 42

In the beginning of our grief, most of us seriously doubt that we will ever fully live again. We knew we would continue to function, to move through each day and interact with others. We knew we still had those who loved us and whom we loved. Still, too much had been lost. We were not whole. Our families were no longer whole either. It seemed impossible to ever think of putting it all back together again. We thought we would be crippled forever. As one young mother told me after a dream she had:

> Grief was like being in a long, dark tunnel without having any idea how long that tunnel was. I crawled along in the dark endlessly, knees sore and my body exhausted.
>
> Then suddenly, I go around a curve and there, way down at the end miles from where I am, is a small glimmer of light. I'm not sure if the light comes from an opening in a crack or if it is really a way out. It doesn't matter at this point. The light represents hope, and I crawled faster toward it.

That tiny speck of light is what keeps us all going. When we are most inconsolable, the light flickers dangerously, almost going out. These are the times we are afraid that we can't hang on—times when we say to ourselves, What's the use? The pain is more than I can bear. Or, I may as well give up. My life doesn't mean anything anyhow. At these times, the darkness almost engulfs us.

LOVE IS WHAT HEALS US

Still we keep on. I believe we keep going because of a major force that connects us to one another. That life-giving force is analogous to the light and the power that motivates us all: love. I believe that love is the guiding force of all life. I believe that the only way we can rebuild our lives after a major disaster is to allow love to heal us. Grief teaches us what real love is about.

So much of our love is conditional, however. We show love to receive love—I'll do this for you if you do that for me. We search for reassurances of love from the important people in our lives. We work hard to get others to love us and not abandon us. But that kind of exchange has its price.

Unfortunately, the more we do for others, the more is expected of us. Disappointments abound as the effort begins to exact fewer rewards. People take for granted the things that we do routinely. In the final analysis, we feel abandoned anyhow. Love that is based on getting is filled with loopholes and disappointments.

If we try to control love, it backfires. Because we find it so hard to open up to others' love, we minimize the love that exists for us in the world. Love means being vulnerable. This is just the opposite of control. It is much easier for most of us to give graciously than to receive graciously. Always giving and never allowing others to give to us, however, is the opposite of love; it is control. Love is offered by opening our hearts, our feelings, and ourselves and never expecting anything in return.

Grief teaches us how love works. During our deepest grief, we are sustained by loved ones who stay near us. If we are lucky, they allow us to express our rage, guilt, and despair without judging us and without expecting anything in return. They show us what love truly means. Their love is the tiny light at the end of the long, dark tunnel. As long as we are open to it, love never disappoints us. And, strangely enough, love grows through suffering, for in suffering we see it without control, without superficiality, and without glitter. Love becomes the major healing element when we have lost a child and find it hard to love ourselves.

Finding ourselves at the turning point puts us in a

dilemma. If we move quickly toward the new beginning, we have to risk changes. There is always the possibility that we will fail—fall on our faces or hate the change. The other alternative, though, is remaining stuck. Staying where we are might appear safe, certainly it is a situation we know, but it is one that keeps us in the quagmire of our guilt. Some choose to stay stuck in bitterness and resentment. Others choose to move on to new beginnings. To me, given these alternatives, there is not really a choice. Who would be content to stay with pain when there is another way of living, a way of living joyfully once again?

FORGIVENESS

Forgiveness works two ways. First, we need to forgive ourselves. After a death, we spend countless hours in anger, guilt, or shame, forever blaming ourselves for somehow being responsible for the death. If we had only done this or if we had been more forceful or less forceful or more watchful, death would never have taken place. Forgiving ourselves is time-consuming. Forgiveness arrives slowly, a little at a time.

Consider the energy the parents in the following cases expended in self-blame:

- Marge blamed herself for being too strict with her seven-year-old son before he died in a school bus accident. She tortured herself by remembering how she expected him to be perfect. "I wanted him to be a good example for his little brother, so he was never allowed to just be a kid. Why couldn't I have seen that? Why did I wait until now to understand?"

- Roger was on Philip's case every minute of the day about taking out the garbage or mowing the lawn. Then, at fourteen, Philip drowned in a nearby lake.

Roger hated himself for focusing on petty household chores and never really getting to know Philip. He thought about all the time he could have been having fun with Philip. He hated himself for that.

- Alice treated Amy's fever at home, thinking Amy had the flu. When symptoms persisted and the doctor was called, it was too late. Spinal meningitis had run its course. Alice wanted to die too.

As parents, we must make decisions all the time about our kids. These decisions are rarely related to a death but, when they are, we must remember that, as parents, we did the best we could with what we had to work with. Until we believe this, we are full of guilt and we block self-forgiveness. After a child dies, it is hard to remember that discipline was necessary and extremely important for his or her well-being. If death hadn't interrupted the progress of our relationships with our children, the relationships would have continued quite naturally and all their various aspects would have created a balanced, nurturing environment.

Forgiveness works the other way too. We need to forgive outside forces for not protecting the child. At first we may rail at God for turning His back for a moment, allowing the child to die. Clara, whose sixteen-year-old son was killed in a car wreck, struggled with her anger at God. She kept the shades drawn; she rarely dressed; and, at certain times when her rage exploded, she went into her yard yelling and shaking her fist at God. It was the only means she had to vent her anger and resentment toward the forces she felt had caused the accident. Yet, for healing to take place, she had to finally let go of her resentments.

Keeping anger alive past the time when anger is no longer helpful only keeps us stuck in our grief. Forgiveness unlocks the past and allows our anger and resentment to dissolve. Once we let go of anger, we are no longer held prisoner by our negative emotions. Our anger can come and go as we find it useful; but once we release our anger, however, we will never be stuck in one place because of it. By surrendering to forgiveness, we can clear the air and make way for fresh beginnings.

FORGETTING

Forgetting means letting go of agonizing reminders surrounding the time of death, of guilt, of shame, of remorse, of anger. This is a hard task, because a parent has a deep commitment to his or her child. The physical separation caused by death has been an agony beyond anything that we could have imagined. Yearning and longing to be with the lost child keeps us tied to him or her in unhealthy ways.

Forgetting doesn't mean that we are to erase all memories. If we were to do that, it would mean denying that the child ever lived. This would not be healthy remembering.

Janine and Robert were able to keep their daughter's memory alive in a healthy way by observing rituals within the family and by acknowledging her life in both public and private ways.

There were seven children all together in their family. Janine had always wanted a lot of kids. She had been brought up in an orphanage and knew the value of belonging to a family. The children were included in all their activities, which suited Robert fine. He loved kids too.

I met this wonderful family shortly after Milly, eighteen, their oldest, was referred to a hospice by their physician. Her cancer had progressed rapidly to the point where her future was being measured in weeks.

Robert and Janine wanted Milly at home. They were determined to keep family members together even through Milly's death, to make them feel a part of the dying.

The kids were in and out of Milly's room whenever she was awake. Even when she was asleep, one or two family members sat with her. Milly wasn't in pain, which helped her remain accessible to her family. Every evening her parents, brothers, and sisters gathered around her bed for a special prayer time. The love that was generated by that family was astounding. I was always lifted by it.

Even so, death was a sad experience. They had been used to being a part of Milly's dying. Now that she was gone, they felt empty and useless. Janine spoke of this:

It felt something like losing a part of you. You get used to having five fingers, then you lop off the thumb and the other fingers feel useless. You can't make them work right. That's the way we felt at first. Milly drew us together and provided a purpose that went beyond our usual life. We missed her so much. It felt empty with her gone, like maybe we should disband or something.

But one night at supper, little Joe, who is only six, said: "Why can't we have our time together at night like we used to? We're still here."

That very night, she said, they resumed the family tradition of gathering. At first the focus was on Milly. Then, gradually, Milly began to take her place among the other six. They began to talk of other things besides Milly.

At Christmas, the whole family made a scrapbook of Milly's things and put it under the tree. They decorated Christmas balls, each one drawing a different figure. There was a Santa Claus on one, a cross on another, an airplane, holly with red berries—whatever came to mind. They were sharing themselves with each other as they had done throughout Milly's illness and death. Milly was remembered in a positive sense while all the sadness connected with her illness and death was slowly erased. The family was able to turn to new experiences, trusting in the future, but keeping Milly alive in a healthy way.

ALLOWING THE NEW PERSON TO EMERGE

How do you live without a part of yourself after an amputation? The answer is you have no choice; you adapt. Adapting to the death of a child is analogous to learning to walk again without a leg. First you depend on a walker, then a crutch, finally a prosthesis. The prothesis takes you to nearly as many places as your leg did, but you know the difference. A change has been made.

As I have emphasized again and again throughout this book, you are never the same after a significant loss. In the early phases of grief, you lose confidence in yourself and in the world. Your trust is badly shaken. Your insecurity is pronounced. As a result, you find it hard to take charge of your life once again. You don't know how to do it or even where to begin.

Your identity used to be based on a life of interacting with your child. In the eyes of the family and community you were the parent of Tim, or Sally, or Judy. You may still be a parent to other children, but not Tim, Sally, or Judy. That one special child is gone, and somehow you must learn to structure your life without him or her. You must find congruence in life without any longer being the parent of that one special child.

There are many steps to discovering the new person you are becoming. Making centering a practice will help move you toward your inner intuitive self, where so many important answers are stored. Getting in touch with the unconscious allows you to access these answers. But, ultimately, leaning on a power greater than yourself will provide the guidance you need. By emptying out the inner buildup of hurt and disappointment, you make room for the incredible power of love and under-standing.

Your new identity can't be rushed. Taking it slowly, a step at a time, is best. You can count on making mistakes now and then that may set you back a little. But discovering your new self is worth it, and you, like everyone, deserves a chance to fulfill your own poten-tial. Your new life will be a combination of both the old and the new. By putting the best parts of them together, you will find the peace and serenity for which you search.

CARING FOR OURSELVES

So few of us know how to nurture ourselves. We can take care of others so much more easily. Yet the child within each of us continues to need security and tender-ness, even though other family members may use up all our reserve of nurturing. Self-nurturing is especially important for those who have lived in nonsupportive environments, those who were damaged by neglect and abuse in early life, for example, or those who grew up in dysfunctional families where they felt emotional or physical abandonment. To nurture ourselves, we may have to unlearn years of faulty thinking—a process that may leave us vulnerable for a time. Stripping down to our vulnerable selves, however, allows us to make new beginnings.

Self-nurturing isn't easy to learn. Most of us don't even know what we need. That's why it is easier to take care of others. We can always meet some other family member's conspicuous needs while leaving our own needs unmet. Yet this eventually leads to disappointments.

Self-nurturing, on the other hand, can be a great adven-ture. If you were told you needed to do one thing for yourself each day for the next month, that it had to be only for you, and that it had to be done alone, would you be able to do it? When I suggest this to clients in therapy who have lived solely for the happiness of others, they are usually unable to think of even one thing offhand. In constantly focusing on others, they have lost the opportunity to nurture and care for themselves. Uncovering gifts we long for takes careful searching.

We need to remember that we are precious gifts to ourselves as well as to others. We deserve love and nurturance and the one way we can ensure receiving them is for each one of us to provide them for ourselves. We need to have patience with ourselves, however, for the habit of self-nurturing doesn't grow overnight.

HOW CAN I LAUGH AGAIN?

This question comes up often and is most likely in the hearts of all bereaved parents at one time or another. The fear of showing pleasure has to do with guilt: guilt at being alive when the child is dead, guilt at the facetious air laughter generates in the face of such solemnity, guilt at what others will think when we don't appear serious. If people see us laughing, perhaps they will think we didn't love our child enough. Let me emphasize, however, that laughter is one of the greatest tension releasers that we know of. Norman Cousins, in his powerful self-disclosing book *Anatomy of an Illness,* tells of the healing properties of laughter. He was able to completely cure his fatal illness with large doses of it. Laughter encourages wellness, and when we allow ourselves the freedom to throw back our heads in spirited laughter, we are involved in a powerful self-healing process.

VACATIONS

Just as we need to release pent-up grief with laughter and pleasure, we need to allow ourselves time away from the ongoing responsibility of work or home tasks. Though it might seem frivolous to take a vacation, some time away could provide a different perspective. If there are other children in the family, getting away together will be most important for family cohesiveness.

Going on vacation may seem like you are leaving your dead child behind. It may not feel right. Allow yourself the grief connected with this step. It is yet another step at closing the circle. As long as you can include your dead child in your plans in a healthy way—such as by talking about how much Johnny would have liked to have seen this or that, for example—and not be overcome with guilt, you are making real progress.

Part of moving on with your life means beginning to live as freely as possible, not encumbered with guilt or shame. Allowing yourself to relax away from home offers more toward healthy recovery than you can realize, and in no way does it deny the love you have for your dead child.

HOLIDAYS

Unlike vacations, which you can choose, holidays come whether you want them or not. For bereaved parents, the family holidays—Thanksgiving, Hanukkah, Christmas—are extremely painful. These are the holidays in which your child participated. There is no getting around it: You will see your dead child everywhere and be poignantly reminded of holidays past.

Because your child will constantly be in your mind and the minds of all the other family members, plan ahead. Get a family consensus about how to memorialize your child. The ritual needn't occupy the center of attention, but it will allow everyone the opportunity to grieve. Openly sharing memories, even if they are painful, will acknowledge the deep and unalterable love the family feels for the missing child.

Holidays take a great deal of psychic energy, so don't

overload yourself. Make sure there are times to rest. Order by catalog. The stores, filled with holiday spirit, are heartbreaking for those who are grieving a dearly loved person.

Allow the whole family to help with holiday preparations. Assign tasks. This way, the remaining children will feel that they have been given the opportunity to be a closer part of the family.

Express your feelings of sadness throughout the holidays and encourage the other family members to do the same. Knowing that you don't have to be stoic all the time releases you to find points of joy in the midst of the sorrow. And you can laugh if you aren't shackled with pent-up tension and guilt.

RE-ENTRY

Meg Johanson came into therapy three years after her married son, Ed, was killed in an accident. He worked for the local power company as a lineman and was electrocuted while repairing a broken line. He had a lovely wife and two beautiful daughters, four and seven. Ostensibly, Meg came in because she was having trouble relaxing. She was an attractive woman of fifty-eight, whose husband had died ten years before. Explaining that she had never been to a therapist before, she talked at length about her problem with tension. I was waiting for a precipitating cause for her inability to relax, but it didn't come . . . until nearly the end of the session.

Meg rather casually said, "Oh yes, there is one more thing. Ed's wife is planning to remarry and move to California." Her face actually became pale as she told me. I knew we had come to the real reason Meg was seeing me that day.

Ed's wife, Charlotte, had been like a daughter to Meg. Because they lived close together, Meg had spent much time caring for Charlotte's girls, Meg's grandchildren. When Charlotte started back to work, Meg kept them during the day. When Ed was killed, Meg and Charlotte grew even closer. Meg tried hard to be there whenever Charlotte needed her. They kept their separate houses, but Meg might as well have lived with her daughter-in-law.

When Charlotte began dating Roger, Meg encouraged her to enjoy herself and have some fun. Even when they talked of marriage, Meg wasn't disapproving. She thought that life would keep on the way it had—she'd take care of the girls as usual. By now, she thought of them as her children.

Then Roger unexpectedly got a transfer. Wedding plans were speeded up, and Roger and Charlotte arranged to marry in a month. Suddenly, for Meg, life came to a halt. Her sole existence was her grandchildren, and the thought of life without them was more than she could bear.

To make matters worse, Charlotte had not asked Meg to move with them as Meg had hoped. Instead, she warmly reiterated that she wanted Meg to visit often. Meg could see what was happening and was heartsick but couldn't bring herself to say anything.

At that point, Meg had a choice. Either she could hibernate forever or she could develop a different life. To Meg the second was enormously frightening. She didn't believe she could do it. Yet, to hibernate seemed like her own personal death.

I wish I could say that the course of therapy moved smoothly and that Meg was ready for re-entry in a short period. This is not the way grief moves. Instead, Meg had many false starts and half-stops when she almost quit. Grief was agony for her at times. Fears would paralyze her. She visited the girls once, swearing she wouldn't do it again because it was too hard and painful to leave them once she was there.

Slowly, however—by sheer grit and extreme courage—
Meg got a job. First she worked part-time and later,
full-time. Even then, however, she tended to spend evenings and weekends alone. She worked to resolve this,
too, finally joining a group of women who went out to
dinner every other week. Later, she learned bridge and
began to play in a large group. She began to receive
invitations for various local events. Life was becoming
more interesting as her focus broadened.

The change in Meg was not on the outer level, although
she did begin to dress with more zip. The real change
took place on the inside—in her willingness to risk, to
try new things and not be afraid that they would be
failures. She had worked successfully on forgiveness with
both her son and Charlotte, letting them go with love.
Now she could see that the change had actually benefited
her by allowing her to become a more independent person. No longer was she just a grandmother clinging to
her grandchildren.

Meg was able to re-enter the world by learning to trust
herself enough to risk changing. Fear filled her at every
turn, but still she courageously continued. I want to add
that Meg did not give up all rights to being a grandmother. The girls were now old enough to visit Meg, and
they often did. Now the three had a new relationship,
however—one that was based on pleasure rather than
on Meg's role as a caregiver.

The greatest serendipity for Meg was that her self-
confidence rose significantly as she had successes in
reaching out to new friends and situations. She saw that
it was through her trust in life that she had created a
fullness of living.

Re-entry isn't easy. After we have lost a child, we feel
more vulnerable than we ever did before. Our confidence
and trust have been badly shattered. We feel different
from others. And we are certain that no one else ever
felt this way before.

Don't think you must jump in with both feet. Take it easy, one day at a time. Start with easy tasks and add to them as you feel more competent. Above all, don't push yourself. Give grief all the time it needs, and make no excuses to anyone. Grief can't be hurried.

HOPE

Each day of our grief brings us a step closer to the peace and serenity we are looking for. Gradually, we are given a little more strength as we continue to accept the reality of the child's death. As we gain greater distance from the death, we begin to observe glimpses of light. At some point, we begin to believe that the struggle to survive this horrible tragedy will one day be over.

Alone, each of us comes to terms with our grief in one way or another. Yet, it helps to know that we are not alone in our suffering, that we haven't been singled out. Somehow it takes a great deal of suffering to integrate the changes necessary for spiritual growth. But the changes are there nevertheless. Grief pushes us to gain a better understanding of the lessons that are there for us to learn.

Through grief, we become wiser, more understanding, more compassionate. Now, more than ever, we can see that the hope of grief lives in the lessons that are there for us, lessons that challenge us to live more authentically; lessons that offer us everyday the opportunity to participate in the adventure of life; and, most important, lessons that encourage us to share our love, our talents, and our special gifts with all who might need them.

11

• • • • • • • • • • • • • • •

Finding Joy
After the Pain

WHEN YOU *are joyous, look deep into your heart and you shall find it is only that which has given you sorrow that is giving you joy.*

When you are sorrowful, look again in your heart, and you shall see that in truth you are weeping for that which has been your delight.

—On Joy and Sorrow
From The Prophet, *by Kahlil Gibran*

When your child has died, you are left feeling empty and alone, different from every other person in the universe. You lose your connection to the world, turning inward to avoid being hurt again. Temporarily stripped, you face the most vulnerable period of your life with little left to stabilize your world. Healing seems improbable.

Yet, you are not without resources. By reaching toward your inner self, searching deeply within, you are given the strength to lift yourself from any dark place. With spiritual guidance you are slowly lifted from suffering to a new place of transcendence.

LETTING GO

As you have learned, you survive the death of a child by finally letting go. You must let go of the child and the many dreams you held for his or her future. You must let go of the old identity you had for yourself before struggling through the ordeal of grief. And finally, you must let go of the fear of reconnecting with the world— a fear that, once you become complacent again, a similar tragedy might strike.

Only in retrospect do you obtain a clear view. You would have given your life for your child. However, once you were faced with the inevitable, you had little choice but to try to get through—an hour at a time, a day, a week. During your deepest grief, you could not recognize how you were changing. You redefined yourself by the choices you made. You had choices to be sure. You chose how you would survive. You could decide whether to remain bitterly cynical, distrusting every change presented to you, or you could confront the lessons of grief and treat them as opportunities for growth. When you have the courage to open yourself to the changes, you chose a triumphant survival.

HEALING THROUGH LOVE

If letting go is what helps us to survive, love is the avenue by which we are healed. As I have said before, I believe that love is the guiding force of all life and when we can finally break away from the dark aspects of fear and resentment, the healing forces of love can mend us.

Love is a gift to be given from our fullness rather than from our emptiness. When we can truly love ourselves, forgiving our shortcomings, accepting our inadequacies, we can truly begin to share our love: No one goes without. Love, then, clears the way for our own healing, smoothing the scars, assuaging the pain.

THE LESSONS OF GRIEF

The lessons of grief will lift us to new levels of living and relating if we accept them. Once learned, we are capable of deeper intimacy, gentle compassion, and a trust in the world that frees us to partake of the adventure of life.

Why is loss such a teacher? It seems that the level of suffering we experience is positively correlated with the opportunity for growth. In other words, the greater the pain, the greater the chance to gain valuable insights.

The lessons of grief can help us build an inner stability and strength so that, when we are confronted with adversity again, we will know, without a shadow of a doubt, that we can both survive and surmount any obstacle. It isn't that loss comes only to teach us. That would be cruel indeed. It is, instead, that when we suffer a loss, we are given the opportunity to open ourselves to change. And it is in our willingness to accept the changes, even embrace them, that the greatest growth is made possible.

There is no question that grief can make us stronger.

Like a broken arm that heals stronger than it was initially, we have the opportunity, through surmounting
our grief, to become much stronger than we were before.
We didn't ask for the tragedy. It was thrust upon us.
We have been left with "whys" we can't answer and pain
of such immense proportions that we feel certain it can
never be healed. Still, stripped of our veneer, we are
compelled to shed our superficiality. Naked, we can begin
to put on the garments that fit us best rather than
drag around the old worn-out clothing that someone else
chose for us. Through grief, we have the opportunity to
become our true selves. It is a time of determining for
ourselves the values that will serve us best as we carve
new identities—the values that will offer us hope for
peace and happiness.

The Value of Friendship

For most of us, the close contact of friends helped us get
through grief. This seems to be universal. When I asked
participants in the Tampa Bereavement Study what
helped them get through grief, almost everyone responded wholeheartedly, "Friends and family." Relationships
were the most valued support.

Grief has taught us how important our friends are, how
much they enrich our lives. Yet we often take our friends
for granted and forget to offer them the attention that
keeps our relationships vital. Grief reminds us that our
friends are special to our growth. When we have close
friends on whom we can rely, we feel safer in the world.
We enjoy the security of belonging to a group. Once we
have grown beyond our own pain, we can befriend other
bereaved persons. Being a part of someone else's pain
and growth can be helpful to ourselves as well as others
because we are then allowed to pass along the love that
was given to us when we so needed it.

Hans Selye, the noted scientist and grandfather of stress research, after years of studying stress and theorizing about it, finally concluded that the most successful way we have of reducing stress in our lives is by adopting what he called altruistic egotism, or earning your neighbor's love. If we do this, he said, we will never be left alone in a crisis and will always have someone to care for us. Having someone who cares is necessary to our growth. It's a form of social insurance that we can store up and collect whenever we need it.

The Importance of Balancing

Grief teaches us how much we need to keep a balanced perspective. So often in the past we focused on our work, our future, our children's activities—with little thought of what we ourselves needed. When we go inward to center ourselves, we have made a valid beginning. When we focus attention on things outside ourselves, we are sharing with our world. One without the other leaves us fragmented, poorly directed. It is in learning to correctly balance ourselves among the interests of our inner and outer lives that we gain the healthiest perspective.

Our personal energy needs to be budgeted just like our finances. There needs to be enough energy to work, love, play, meditate, and nurture ourselves and others. Basic to all this is the correct balance. Doing one thing too long makes us stale, robs us of energy and enthusiasm. As we have learned during the exhausting days of grief, we have time and energy for limited activities only. Balancing keeps us properly centered.

The Need to Take Life a Day at a Time

We used to feel we had some control over our lives. We lived in the future with our plans. We worried about where our children would go to college, how we could afford it, would our children's grades get them in a good school, what would they do afterward, and so on. These are important issues, of course, but if they are the primary focus we miss the best part of today. We know now that we can't control the future. Grief has taught us the importance of living each moment, each day as it comes, accepting that our Higher Power will guide us. When we live in the future, the precious moments of today slip by unnoticed. On the other hand, when we stay in the moment, we experience all that is available from life. We become one with all that is happening around us.

All we really have of life is this present moment. It needs our undivided attention. If we miss the moment, we'll miss the invitation to grow, to help a friend, laugh with our child, or share a cherished time with our mate. The present holds all we need—all we'll ever need—for our happiness.

The Need to Accept Life's Challenges

We've already met the toughest challenge we'll ever meet. We have lost a precious child. Inherent in this one major loss are a myriad of challenges. We can resist them and remain stuck in bitterness and self-pity, but in doing this we abdicate our chance to grow, to learn, and to find ultimate peace. Our challenges beckon us toward the stronger person we can grow to be. Our challenges are our gifts. They show us that we are ready to move ahead to new awarenesses. Challenges demand that we turn to others for help rather than stay in compulsive self-reliance. We invite others to share the load. Challenges force us to accept changes we never would have tackled. We learn to risk.

At any time in our lives, we either grow or regress.

There is no in-between. Fear often keeps us on the fence, afraid to move forward and afraid to retreat. Remember that fear comes from a lack of faith in the universe. In making personal changes, we are required to jump into an abyss and trust that a power greater than ourselves will be there to catch us. When we truly let go, guidance and support are there.

Thankfully, we are never without challenges. They are gifts to grow on. Each time we risk opening a new door, we can be assured that we will find a solution—perhaps not the one we were seeking, but a valuable reward nonetheless. But it is equally important to first close the door on yesterday so that we will be ready to move forward.

THE IMPORTANCE OF HONESTY

So many of us have lived our lives trying to please others, worrying about what they thought, wondering if they approved of us. As a result, we gave them what they wanted. We told them what they wanted to hear. Worst of all, we behaved as they wanted us to behave and lost ourselves in the exchange.

Our grief at losing a child put us in touch with what is real, what truly matters to us. Stripped down, we found another way of being. We began to see the value and importance of being our own persons. We learned that we can acknowledge what matters for us and be true to that ideal.

To live honestly, we must be free to speak our own hearts. Our values and our realities come from our own experiences, and our spiritual well-being invites us to be true to them. Strength and growth will come from validating ourselves. Yesterday, in deep grief, we doubted our value to society and even to our family and friends. But today, as we begin to establish our new identities, we need speak only what is true for us. When we can do this, we find harmony both within ourselves and within the universe.

Honesty is also the key to true intimacy. Intimacy means self-disclosure, of becoming more open with others. It means revealing to another person our deepest secrets, our shame and guilt, and holding nothing back.

The deepest level of emotional honesty is required for true intimacy. But when we can create it, nothing can penetrate the bond. We validate ourselves and the other person when we risk true intimacy.

The Importance of Humility

In our culture, humility is often seen as a weak trait. It is thought that the humble person is on the low end of the totem pole. Ego, on the other hand, pushes us to be more aggressive, to take on the virtues that society embraces. Ego puts us in constant stuggle, competing for a better position professionally and socially, competing to have more material possessions than our neighbors, competing to do things better than others. These acts of competition often push us to behavior we're not proud of. The struggles we have within ourselves and with other people take their toll on us. Eventually they can trigger either physical or emotional lapses.

In losing a child we were forced to a place of humility. We lost all control over our world and, when our frustration and anger brought no relief, we had to succumb to the intolerable knowledge that the child was gone. Our egos couldn't help us.

Humility is the smoother way to live. When we can learn the way of cooperation, we see that by bowing with the wind we can ease our journey. Part of the process of grief is in accepting the changes that take place. When we can slide by the negative situations that confront us, we free our energy to flow with the positives. We need never be thwarted by people or situations because the barriers that stand in our way can strengthen our reliance on a Higher Power. Our lives become smoother because of our growing trust. Living in humility, nothing is demanded of us, and we are free to chart our own course in cooperation with God and our fellow human beings.

The Value of Lightheartedness

Certainly, we have had our heavy times. There were days when we needed all our strength simply to endure, to live from one moment to the next. Life deals wounds that are hard to heal. Yet, when we can muster a lighthearted look, even for a moment, we help ourselves.

We sometimes fall into the trap of taking ourselves so seriously that we attach great weight to our every move. Lightheartedness is a wonderful tool for releasing that weight. In addition, sharing lighthearted play is often the only way to touch another person. When we do this we don't feel so isolated or lonely.

Lightheartedness doesn't mean carelessness. Instead it becomes a gift to the human spirit—especially when that spirit is burdened with sorrow. Laughter in the midst of our pain gives us strength to continue and offers perspective when the going is hard.

The Importance of Appreciation

Grief teaches us the importance of appreciation. We are aware of the things we wished we had said or done when we had the chance. There may have been gifts we planned to make, letters we wanted to write, love we meant to express. Because we are prone to procrastination, we put things off, thinking there will be another day. Grief teaches us that time is not on our side and that each small appreciation we can show today is a guarantee that what we appreciate will not go unacknowledged.

When we show appreciation to others, we not only embrace them but improve our own self-image. The good feelings that accompany the transaction tend to rub off on us. In showing appreciation, we have an opportunity to help one another as we ourselves grow in self-love.

The Value of Being Flexible

When we were children we could afford to be flexible, spontaneous. Someone else was in charge. Our parents set the limits, and we were permitted to move about within the space provided, without thinking too much about schedules. As we grew older and accepted responsibility, we took on more control until we were laden down with both responsibility and control. There wasn't time for spontaneity; everything needed to be scheduled. Our flexibility was lost in the web of serious adulthood.

Grief has taught us the need to break down rigid living. The more flexible our lives, the more easily we can participate in the serendipity that life continually offers. An unscheduled walk in the woods on a beautiful fall afternoon, a sudden decision to bundle the children up for a toboggan run during the first snow, sneaking out of work to catch an afternoon movie you've wanted to see forever, accepting a last-minute invitation to a ball game on a Saturday when there is work piled up: All these show flexibility, but they also are great indicators that the child inside you is alive and eager to show you some of the special pleasures you deserve.

A rigid way of living makes us old before our time. On the other hand, getting old is always before our time.

If we remain flexible, spontaneous, and able to seize
the moment for fun, we will never grow old no matter the
number of years.

The Importance of Faith

Our concept of the meaning of life was shaken when we
lost our child. We were required to keep going anyway,
having no idea where life could lead. Most of us lived
in a vacuum those first few months. Raw pain was all
we knew. Gradually, as the mists began to clear, we
wondered how we ever made it. Though we didn't always
accept that a Higher Power was supporting us, we do now.

Denying faith makes us bitter. It fosters resentments
and self-pity. It keeps us stranded and stuck in the third
phase of grief, conservation/withdrawal, where we are
afraid to move, afraid of life.

Having faith in a power greater than ourselves sus-
tains us. Because grief is so filled with fear, without a
faith in some higher spiritual source, we become lost in
an angry sea of anxiety and depression. We are afraid
to make decisions, we are terrified for the safety of our
children, our mate, our world. We realize how few things
there are that we can actually control.

As we grow stronger, we learn that all difficulties are
truly opportunities for exceptional growth and that with
faith we can accept challenges without fear. We can let go
of our problems. It is my belief that we don't have to worry about circumstances, for we are always watched over.

FINDING JOY

The lessons of grief will lead us to a new joy for living
if we allow them. So much will depend on the level of
intimacy we've grown comfortable with as we shared our

grief, our fears, and our successes with others. We also have a responsibility to ourselves. Alone, we need to come to full acceptance of the loss, the turmoil, and the trauma we've experienced.

Grief changes us but, if we can trust our inner urgings to direct us, we will not go far afield. Adopting a new identity, however, is not easy. Suddenly reacting to a situation in a way we never did before surprises and perplexes us. One bereaved parent said:

> Before I lost Angela, I was very outgoing. I loved people. I loved parties—both going to and giving them. I always liked being on committees—belonging, I guess. Now, I don't know what's happened to me. I want more time for myself. Committee work tires me but, I hate to admit it, it also bores me. I don't even like most parties now. I'd rather be with only a few good friends. It kind of scares me. I'm afraid I'm becoming too closed in.

What is happening to this young woman is that, out of her grief, she is developing a new persona; one that is based on similar values but a different style. She still likes people, but she has learned to appreciate herself more and guards her quiet time. She recognizes the need to balance her energy so she doesn't push herself into areas that don't interest her. Large parties seem superficial now that she has confronted grief and seen the need to be honest and open.

Allowing the change to take place without pressure from without or force from within will gradually unveil your new self. When it comes from the center of your being, your joy will show in all areas of your life.

WE HAVE LEARNED GREATER COURAGE

I remember meeting with a wonderful woman in her early eighties whose husband and son had died only three years apart. I was conducting a follow-up interview to see how she was doing around sixteen months after the last death. As we sat down to talk she asked, "Did I tell you about my son's death?" I answered, "Yes, you told me about him when I visited last, and I'm so sorry." She said, "No, not that son. Another son died two months ago of cancer." This woman had survived the death of not only her husband of fifty-two years but also two sons as well.

I was amazed at her remarkable courage and asked her how she kept going in light of such heavy losses. She told me that her son left two teenage children of his own and they spent a great deal of time with her. "I have them to take care of now. We are planning a vacation together somewhere this summer. We haven't exactly decided where, but I know I'll have a good time with them." This courageous woman was neither hiding from herself nor the world. She was meeting it head on, making sure each day was valuable. I'm sure she had many down days too, yet, she courageously adjusted to the changes that were taking place.

We often reserve the word *courage* for people working in life-threatening situations: fire-fighters, soldiers on the battlefield, and the like. Courage can appear in situations that seem less dramatic. It takes enormous courage to adapt to changes after the death of a significant person, to risk moving on in a world that has become empty because that one special person is no longer there. We need to recognize our own courage at surviving and turning our loss into a growth experience.

WE HAVE LEARNED TO LET GO

We have learned to let go of so many things, people, conditions, and places. Each one held poignant memories, but the struggle to hang on to any part of them clouds the present. If we are still looking back over our shoulders, we will miss what is here for us now. Hanging on to lost attachments prolongs our pain. By letting them go, we make room for new experiences, new opportunities.

We rarely opt to let go unless we have to. It has often been said that we go kicking and screaming to our growth. Suffering is not the way we would choose to learn these lessons, but the end result is that our new experiences push us beyond the selves we used to be to a place of deeper compassion for others and a better understanding of our new lives.

WE HAVE LEARNED THE IMPORTANCE OF REACHING OUT

We are each traveling our own special pathways. When we can connect even for a moment and savor that moment, our lives will be enriched by the encounter. We are all teachers and we are all students needing information each has to share. Our journeys are not the same, but our destination is. We need never take another step alone.

Reaching out to others after we have been helped through our grief allows us to acknowledge the lessons we have learned and, at the same time, pass that wisdom on to other bereaved persons.

WE HAVE LEARNED DEEPER COMPASSION

By traveling together on the same paths, we have shared the suffering of others, while our own pain has given us a deeper understanding of what others might be feeling. We become more open to sharing our lives with those who may need our help. When we recognize that there are no accidents, that others are brought into our life for a purpose, we are able to welcome them with a sense of warmth and compassion that we never experienced before. Being aware of our own Higher Power, we connect with the Higher Power in others.

WE SEEK A QUIETER HARMONY IN LIFE

We have learned much about the importance of letting life flow rather than trying to direct it. When we can do this, more of our attention is released to watch each day unfold. We miss fewer of the day's events; therefore, we are able to celebrate all the serendipitous surprises and adventures life offers us. We grow in better understanding of our own unfolding as we allow our Higher Power full partnership in the venture.

Harmony also grows as a result of feelings of gratitude. We may still experience twinges of grief and shame. There are days when we might be too afraid to show gratitude for fear the other shoe will fall—that if we become too lax, tragedy will strike again. These thoughts are barriers to our growth, for they interfere with our ability to accept the good things of life. Gratitude is what prepares us for the blessings that are waiting for us. The more in tune we are with the spiritual activity around us, the more harmonious each day will be.

WE HAVE LEARNED THE
VALUE OF SERENITY

When we are young, the thought of serenity seems too passive. It even sounds boring. Only with maturity and experience do we learn the full meaning of serenity, and so come to value it as an important way of life.

In early grief, however, we were far from serene. We felt restless. It was a restlessness born of the frustration of searching for the lost child and not finding him or her—of focusing attention on getting him or her back without hope for retrieval. Over time, we were forced to surrender our efforts to a power greater than ourselves and allow that power to guide us to our inner reservoir of spiritual strength. Many of us didn't even realize we had such resources. Only then, however, could we finally acknowledge our loss and let go of our child as well as our old identity.

In solitude we find serenity. We receive assurance from our inner guide that all is well, that our way is being lighted. Gradually it will become natural to turn within for answers and assurances.

WE ARE BLESSED THROUGH OUR SPIRITUAL GROWTH

We have struggled through the phases of grief, feeling they would never end. At times, we hung onto the pain because we feared the emptiness of not feeling at all. Yet, as our faith grew, as we trusted more and more that there was a power greater than ourselves seeing us through, we came to a better understanding of the process of grief. We understand that the pain of the present opens the way to the serenity of the future.

In my book, *Surviving Grief and Learning to Live Again,* I wrote of the need to outline a sixth phase of grief, that of spiritual growth. The feeling that we have not taken theory far enough until we incorporate spiritual fulfillment into the phases is still persistent. Moreover, everyone might not wish to enter this phase. We all have a different cadence to our growth as well as a different focus for our lives. Because our spiritual journey moves in the right tempo for each of us, and because the journey goes on for a lifetime and beyond, we can rest assured that we are in the right place at the right time. We can feel confident that we are well guided and given all the wisdom and knowledge we need—at every moment.

You are not the same person you were before your child's death. You have changed. Moreover, while your child has been in your heart every step of the way, he or she has changed as well. From the raw painful memories of early grief, when you dealt with sharp photographic images of your child, you have shifted to the softer, more distant, picture of a lovingly remembered son or daughter. From time to time a deep dull ache in your heart reminds you of your loss, but the intense suffering is past now. As you changed, you have been healed and renewed by the loving presence of a Higher Power.

The spiritual journey is not without pitfalls. When you lose a child, it takes effort to redevelop faith. Your trust was so badly damaged that it will take much positive practice to gain the confidence to risk again. Yet, in going within, centering yourself, you are supplied the strength, courage, and confidence that allows you to begin to live again.

And you can have joy. Joy awaits all of us, but we must be open to it. We must be willing to let go of the suffering and take hold of life once again. We need to trust that the most difficult circumstances won't ever keep joy from us. Having learned the lessons that grief offers us, we can tap our spiritual resources and gain strength each time we meet adversity.

Joy and sorrow can be compared to the ebb and flow of the ocean tide. They are natural rhythms and, as such, both are valuable. True joy comes not from giddy, superficial excitement as we may have known it before; instead, it comes from a deeper place of courage and compassion, where sorrow and grief are nurtured. Together, joy and sorrow supply the richness for our growth, add depth and dimension to our lives, and beckon us on to seek and find true peace and serenity for our souls.

> You are the bows from which your children as
>   living arrows are sent forth.
> The archer sees the mark upon the path of
>   the infinite and He bends you with His
>   might that His arrows may go swift and far.
> Let your bending in the archer's hand be for
>   gladness;
> For even as He loves the arrow that flies, so
>   He loves also the bow that is stable.
>   —On Children
>   From *The Prophet,* by Kahlil Gibran

12

. . . .

How We Can Help Ourselves

WE WERE thrown into grief so fast that we didn't know what hit us. We didn't know how to act . . . we were like zombies just wandering around trying to hold it together. Later on, we tried to figure out how we were supposed to act. How could we know even what to expect? We'd never been through this before. We'd never even imagined it before.

—Bereaved father, age 28

Our needs as bereaved parents vary greatly between the first phase and the last. Because of this, I have listed suggestions for help according to phase. Though many of the items listed will help at any time, some of these suggestions are specific to the cited phase.

To resolve a significant loss experience, it is necessary first that we acknowledge the loss; then let go of the beloved person; adjust to a new world without the lost person; and, finally, accept the vast changes in our own identity. As I have emphasized throughout this book, grief is a time- and energy-consuming process. It can't be hurried.

PHASE 1: SHOCK

During the time we are experiencing it, recognizing the amount of shock we are feeling is difficult. So often we try to negate our feelings and try to stay in tight control. This phase of grief is frightening because we feel the world has suddenly gone out of control and we are left hanging onto nothing. However, remaining stoic and closed off emotionally does more harm than good. A healthier response is to give in to your true emotions, without feeling ashamed or embarrassed.

- Acknowledge the pain you are feeling. This is no time for bravery. Others may compliment you for being "strong," but that is because it makes them feel better—not you.
- Allowing others to comfort and nurture you is extremely important. Because of the degree of shock you are experiencing, you will be beset with confusion. The things you can usually figure out quite readily might now seem monumental. Your mind is like a kaleidoscope of fast-moving images. Nothing makes sense.

- Don't be afraid to ask for what you need. Others may be timid about offering help, thinking that they are intruding. In addition, most people are at a loss as to what to say or do, since their experience with this particular devastating loss is minimal. They will probably be relieved and gratified if you can suggest something helpful for them to do, though relieving and gratifying others is not your job.

- This may be the most frightening experience of your life. You have an enormous need for safety. Your world has just exploded, and you are trying to make meaning out of it all. The sheer helplessness of the loss makes you feel like a child needing the safety of a strong parent. Keep those nearest and dearest to you as close as possible.

- You may have never had a death experience prior to this, so you may feel unequipped to contribute to the funeral arrangements. However, any small involvement in the plans will be a comfort to you later. By simply selecting an appropriate hymn, a special reading that meant something to your child, or asking a close friend to speak, you can make the services more personal. Studies have shown that parents of small children and infants, in particular, were greatly helped in their grief by being able to dress their dead child. This job isn't for everyone; if you find it impossible, don't worry. Only a small percentage of parents can manage to do this.

- Truly believing that your child has died will be difficult, even though you are well aware of the facts. Things around you will seem unreal. Be patient with yourself. It will take a long time to process this tragic event.

- Because of the shock you are undergoing, you may experience one or several symptoms that seem unusual: dryness of the mouth, a need to sigh often, uncontrollable trembling, the tendency to startle easily, nausea, or sleep disturbance. These are all reactions to your body's alarm system, which has been thrown into a state of emergency. These symptoms will pass in time and are a normal response to shock.

- Getting through the rituals and the first few months of grief will take all the energy and strength you can muster. Rest is imperative. If you can't sleep, perhaps a mild tranquilizer will help. Don't hesitate to ask your doctor for something to help. There is no need to fear addiction if you follow your physician's orders and use the drug only as necessary.

PHASE 2: AWARENESS OF LOSS

The second phase of grief is marked by intense separation anxiety. By now, you are fully aware intellectually of what has happened but are still far from emotional acknowledgment. You may feel on the edge of a nervous breakdown much of the time, barely holding it together. The feeling of being out of control is stronger even than during the previous phase. You feel separated from everything you hold dear.

The main task during this phase is to fully experience the pain. Though it may seem easier to block off negative emotions such as anger or guilt, in the long run doing so will thwart your eventual healing by stuffing these feelings deep inside.

- Keep talking about your child. As it is, you probably have little else on your mind, so verbalize your thoughts. Try not to worry about what others are thinking about this. Right now, it is your grief and it is extremely important to validate yourself and your child.

- Give yourself permission to cry without apology. What could be more natural? Your heart has been broken. Of course you need to cry. Besides, by showing others your tears, you give them permission to cry as well.

- Your anger may well up either consistently or only from time to time. You may feel disproportionate anger in regard to the small irritations that affect you throughout the day. These are normal outlets for the frustration and inner turmoil you feel at being deprived of your child.

- The death of a child produces large amounts of guilt and shame. You will find areas to feel guilty about no matter how exemplary you were as a parent. The best way to deal with both guilt and shame is to talk about them with trusted friends or a grief counselor. When you can normalize your feelings of guilt, you are in a better position to let them go. Guilt and shame, when not aired, tend to slow the healing process.

- This phase is marked by prolonged stress. Your body is pumping extra adrenaline to balance the seesaw effect of emotional outbursts. It takes a lot of energy to cry or to feel rage, guilt, or intense yearning. Just at a time when you probably couldn't care less about yourself, the need for special attention is greatest. Systematic exercise and a balanced diet are extremely important to ensure that you stay well.

- During this phase, you will probably experience an exaggerated fear that shows itself in your anxiety over other family members' well-being and even your own. This is typical of separation anxiety; it will pass when you can rebuild some trust in the world.

- You may tend to overreact to the least slights. Don't be alarmed. Your personality has not changed permanently. Your oversensitivity won't last. It is part of grief paranoia resulting from the fear of lack of safety. However, in overreacting to others, you may push away the support you need. Talk your reactions over with your friends and try to clear the air on the spot. You have enough to deal with without taking on added resentments.

- If your mate isn't showing the same symptoms of grief that you are, try to understand. Men and women grieve differently. Besides, we don't all follow the same time sequence in moving through the phases of grief. Listen to him or her without judging how they are processing their grief. Trust that your partner is surviving in his or her own way.

- Show appreciation to the friends who stick by you. You need them now, and support is a two-way street. Moreover, showing appreciation will lift your own spirits some.

- You feel that your loss makes you different from everyone in the world. You may think no one can possibly understand what you are feeling. This is why it is so important to find a self-help group such as The Compassionate Friends. Everyone who attends has lost a child. Though each person's experience is different, the feelings group members share will be quite similar to yours. You won't feel so alone anymore.

- If groups make you uncomfortable and your support system is not helping, find a grief counselor who understands the process of bereavement. You have just been through the worst, most tragic experience any parent can live through. You deserve help.

PHASE 3: CONSERVATION/WITHDRAWAL

According to most researchers, this is the worst phase of grief. Phase 3 feels more like depression than any other phase. You withdraw and need to be alone a great deal. Yet, this pulling in is actually a positive, adaptive move. You are, in fact, attempting to recover energy lost during the first two phases of grief. Only by re-energizing can you accomplish the work necessary to resolve grief.

The main task of phase 3 is to accept the reality of the loss and determine how you will handle grief: whether by growing or by regressing.

- To accept reality, you must have the courage to look reality in the face. The third phase allows you this time. Dealing with your child's death takes courage and you can't do it when you are distracted by others. Give yourself permission to withdraw.

- Phase 3 is a period when you need more sleep than before. Your body is coming off the excess adrenaline supply, and you need to conserve what energy you can. Take naps when you can and try to get at least eight hours of solid sleep at night. You will probably need more like nine or ten.

- If you haven't had the courage to look at photographs of your child, now is the time to take them out and go through each one. You may want to put together a scrapbook of your child's life. If there are no photographs, you can gather whatever you have to either frame or place all together in a small box. Having your child's name on the top will further memorialize him or her.

- You have not only lost your child, but a large part of yourself as well. Allow yourself time to mourn both the child and the way of life that was.

- Nurture yourself with special favors: good food, a small bouquet of flowers, a favorite cologne, a visit to an art gallery. This is a period for regaining your strength, and you need to nourish yourself however you can.

- Simplify everything in your life. Find shortcuts for

tasks, and realize that much of what you think you "should" do is useless activity anyhow. In phase 3, conserve energy so that you can gather strength for the next phase.

- Allow plenty of time for phase 3. Don't let others talk you into overdoing when you know good and well that you really feel like taking it easy.

- Think about how you want to live your life. As you let go of your old life, a new way of being begins to take shape as a distinct possibility. You have the opportunity to know what really matters to you. You must decide if you have the courage to carry through on your desires.

This is a low period but things will get better. They won't be this way forever, I promise.

PHASE 4: HEALING

This phase marks the turning point in grief. The previous phase has given you rest so that you have regained energy. You note small advances in your ability to assume control over your life again. Your beloved child is still very much in your thoughts, but you are working through forgiveness during this phase.

As you learn to forgive yourself, you are ready to accept a new identity. You have the task in this phase of closing the circle on your past. The life you lived before is no longer accessible. It is time to carve out for yourself an identity that suits you today.

- As healing imperceptibly begins and you relinquish your child emotionally, allow yourself time off from your grief. Find pleasurable things to do, and let go of the needless guilt that has clogged your life. Pleasure is healthy and healing.

- There will be little lifts in energy here and there. Recognize that they are like guideposts pointing to a resolution to grief. There is an end to the suffering, and it is in sight.

- Learning to let go of painful reminders of your child's death takes time and patience. As you can release them, however, you find that sad memories are replaced by memories of happier times when your child was joyous and well. When you can do this, you will have conquered much of your grief by turning memories of your child into healthy remembering.

- If you haven't already, begin a systematic exercise program. It is the regularity of exercise that makes it truly beneficial. The long, fallow period of grief has probably left you in need of muscle tone and cardiovascular rejuvenation.

- Revamp your diet to decrease fat and replace it with fruits and vegetables. Eating a balanced diet is similar to a balanced exercise program. Remember the four food groups—they are just as important for you as they were for your child.

- Begin making more decisions for yourself. Grief has made you tenuous in deciding certain conditions for your life. For a while you probably became unsure of your potential. Be courageous, however, and don't be afraid of mistakes now and then. One thing is for sure: No one is perfect. Accepting your mistakes is a part of growth.

- Reach out to others. Coming out of the dark tunnel of grief makes you cautious to be sure, but there are other bereaved parents out there who need your help and wisdom.

- Find a new interest, hobby, or sport. As part of your self-discovery program, a new activity is a hands-on way to investigate new possibilities for your life.

- Take time to center. This is the best way to discover the new direction you want to make. By centering, you have the opportunity to find yourself and open yourself to all sorts of possibilities.

PHASE 5: RENEWAL

The last phase of bereavement moves you to a new level of functioning. You have come through a death experience. As a part of your old life dies, you prepare for a rebirth into a new one. You have survived the agonizing loss of your child, gained strength in the process, and developed a new courage that helps you accept full responsibility for the person you are becoming.

You are aware that there will always be poignant moments of remembering: anniversary reactions when you don't expect them, loneliness at times for both your child and the life you have had to leave behind. But you have been given an opportunity to learn the lessons of grief, an opportunity to grow emotionally as well as spiritually.

The task of the fifth phase of grief is to develop a new persona, to accept full responsibility for your own happiness, and to learn to live in a way that reflects your true self.

- Continue to include memories of your child in your discussions with family and friends. There will be times when you are asked how many children you have. Don't be afraid to tell others about your child. I used to hesitate to disclose Jim's death, because it made everyone so uncomfortable. But leaving him out made me uncomfortable. Healthy remembering is a positive side of grief, and we need to practice healthy remembering as often as it seems appropriate.

- It may be a good time to plan a ritual of renewal. Actually, a ritual at every phase of grief would be most helpful. (See Chapter 8 on rituals for ideas.) I urge you to recruit the help of your mate and children when planning a ritual unless it is one you want to be especially your own. Joining the family together solidifies your relationships while linking you into a stronger family unit.

- Through your grief you have changed. Your mate has changed as well. Keep active communication going in order to stay in touch with the new person each of you is becoming. When you can change and grow together, you strengthen your marriage immeasurably.

- Your friends won't know that you have changed. There is a tendency for others to try to place you back the way you were most familiar to them. Verbalize your new feelings to let everyone know the way your thoughts and behavior have changed. If you are not sure what you think yet or how you really want to be, verbalize that too. When you open yourself, you validate yourself and give credence to your right to change and grow.

- You have learned about centering and now you can begin to put some of your new goals into practice. This takes focusing, however, but is absolutely necessary to actualize the new persona.

There is no scheduled time sequence to the grief process. No one can say how long any particular individual will take to resolve a significant bereavement. Having experienced the worst thing that could ever happen, it is imperative that you give yourself all the time you need to come through the entire process. If you try to hurry grief, you will miss the opportunities that are there for your learning.

Nothing could ever make up for the terrible loss you experienced as the result of your child's death. But if you miss the lessons that the loss holds for you, there will be nothing positive to reclaim after all.

13

. . . .

For Friends and Family Members: Providing the Best Support

I WISH I had known what to say. I mean a whole month went by before I could even get up my nerve to call her. I tried to think of what I'd be feeling if something happened to one of my children, but it was too horrible to even imagine. But I wish I'd gone to see her sooner. I just couldn't.

—Neighbor of a bereaved mother

Supporting someone whose child has just died is difficult
for anyone to contemplate. The loss is so enormous that
we have few words of comfort to offer. But remember:
Though you won't be able to change the way a grieving
parent feels by what you say or do, you will add immea-
surable comfort to their lives by simply being there.

Many times what we say can actually hinder rather
than help. Using a trite or untrue statement such as "I
know how you feel" can anger a grieving person and
bring much discomfort. Only the bereaved know how
they truly feel. Especially after the death of a child, when
parents and immediate family members feel so different
from everyone else, suggesting familiarity with their
feelings is inappropriate.

There are two categories of caring: external caring and
internal caring. External caring is analagous to sympathy. It represents a typical problem-solving approach
and is often seen as manipulative.

External caring says, "I recognize your plight. I see
you are different in your struggle. I see you are going
through a rough time, but I am not you. I do not have
to go through this—you do. I will help if you ask me,
but I will not intrude on your pain—it is yours, not mine.
I will solve your problems for you as long as they are
short-term. Otherwise, I have my own problems to take
care of."

Internal caring is a more nurturing way to approach
a person. As such, it is more in line with empathy than
sympathy. Internal caring says, "I am hurting with you.
I see your pain, and I know you hurt. Though I do not
know exactly what you are feeling, I do know your grief
is most serious. I will be here to support you. I will not
judge. I will love you all the while, respect the struggle
you are going through, and admire your courage and
supply what strength I can for you. You are given no
choice in this matter but, if more than one person shares
the pain, it will help. I will not offer advice unless you

ask and then I will offer it only tentatively. I recognize your need to maintain control over your life."

There are many helpful things you can do for the bereaved, especially soon after the death. Don't ask the grieving person what you can do, just do it. The bereaved parent will not be able to think what needs to be done. Carry your tasks through quietly.

1. Offer to write or call out-of-town friends who haven't heard about the death yet.
2. Bring over meals or special dishes. Your thoughtfulness in preparing something will be deeply appreciated.
3. Go to the grocery store for the bereaved family.
4. Offer to take care of small children.
5. Answer the phone.
6. Wash the car and fill it with gas.
7. House-sit.
8. Vacuum and clean the house.
9. Wash towels and bed linens or anything else that needs it.
10. Mow the grass or rake leaves.
11. Send a sympathy letter and include any memories you have of the child. Emotionally, that child is still alive to the parents and reminders of special remembrances are tremendously important for them.

After the funeral:

1. Offer to address thank-you cards.
2. Invite the bereaved parents to have coffee, tea, or something stronger.
3. Take them to breakfast or lunch.
4. Offer to go to the cemetery with them.

5. Take a small flowering plant or bouquet.

6. Help sort the child's belongings.

7. Taxi the children to lessons.

8. Continue to do the things mentioned in the first list.

9. Continue phoning or visiting, but always, always arrange a visit ahead of time.

10. Invite them to go on short junkets. Keep outings short and simple because the strength of those in grief is tenuous.

- Don't minimize the bereaved's grief by relating your own stories of death and sickness. Offering clichés such as "Aren't you glad you had him for ____ number of years" only angers grieving parents.

- It isn't necessary to say a great deal on an initial visit. A warm hug can convey more than words can ever say. They only need to know you are there with them in love and caring.

- Bereaved parents are thinking of nothing else but their dead child. Any attempt to distract the griever by talking of trivia may result in resentment on their part. Talking about superficial things seems to minimize their loss.

- Be a nonjudgmental listener. Do not offer advice about how they should think or feel. We are all unique and every bereavement is different.

- If the bereaved parent cries, don't try to change the subject or encourage them not to cry. Friends of a bereaved person often feel that, if the bereaved person begins to cry, they must have caused the tears by saying or doing something insensitive. Don't worry; the grief is always present, and you can't make it worse. Besides, tears are healing. The bereaved needs friends who won't turn away from their tears.

- The bereaved also need friends who won't be shocked by their anger or judge it. Anger is a natural response to the frustration and helplessness the grievers are feeling.
- As grief continues through months (or even years), don't leave the bereaved or discontinue your support. Their suffering will be long and agonizing. Your presence, in whatever capacity, will be a solid support for them as they move toward resolution.

14

• • • • • • • • • • • • • •

Self-Help Organizations: Lifelines

American Association of Suicidology (AAS)
2459 South Ash St.
Denver, CO 80222
(303) 692-0985

AAS can supply information to lead families of suicide victims
to local resources such as survivors' groups, literature about
suicide, and other help for the bereaved.

The Candlelighters Childhood Cancer Foundation
1901 Pennsylvania Ave. NW, Suite 101
Washington, DC 20006
(202) 659-5136

This organization is devoted to supporting parents of children
who have or who have had cancer. They are led by the philosophy that "It is better to light one candle than to curse the
darkness." From the beginning of diagnosis throughout treatment and on to either cure or death, these parents support
each other through their time of need. The Candlelighters
Childhood Cancer Foundation has groups meeting throughout
the world. There are no dues, and the bimonthly newsletter
is free as well.

Child Find of America, Inc.
P.O. Box 277
New Paltz, NY 12561
(914) 255-1848

Child Find assists parents in finding their missing children. It also offers counseling services for families of missing children. The group sponsors a toll-free hotline for calls from people who have seen an advertised photograph and think they have seen a missing child. The hotline number is 1-800-I-AM-LOST.

The Compassionate Friends (TFC)
Box 3696
Oak Brook, IL 60522-3696
(708) 990-0010

TCF has been a cornerstone for bereaved parents throughout the United States as well as internationally. TCF welcomes bereaved parents of all ages to simply come and be a part of the group. There is no pressure to talk; many parents only listen for the first few meetings, usually feeling more comfortable about sharing later on. The major advantage, of course, is having the opportunity to tell and to listen to each other's stories over and over. This self-help volunteer organization currently has 655 chapters in the United States. There are no dues, and joining is only a matter of being there.

Concerned United Birthparents, Inc.
Attn: J. Fenton
Machinists Building
2000 Walker
Des Moines, IA 50317
(515) 262-9120

This organization provides mutual support for birth parents who must give their babies up for adoption. The need of these birth parents is to be recognized as parents who may grieve as intensely as those who have lost a child through death. For information, send $1 plus a self-addressed business-size envelope to the preceding address.

Mothers Against Drunk Driving (MADD)
Attn: Inquiries Dept.
669 Airport Frwy., Suite 310
Hurst, TX 76053
(817) 268-6233

The major goal of MADD is educating the public about the dangers of drunk driving. The group provides information to national media and offers brochures, bumper stickers, buttons, and pamphlets. MADD works for the enactment of stronger laws against drivers who drink. A quarterly newsletter keeps readers abreast of current events and legislative action.

National SIDS Clearinghouse
8201 Greensboro Dr., Suite 600
McLean, VA 22102
(703) 821-8955

The Clearinghouse offers helpful literature on sudden infant death syndrome (SIDS), including reports on the latest medical research.

National Sudden Infant Death Foundation
2 Metro Plaza, Suite 205
8240 Professional Pl.
Landover, MD 20785
(800) 211-SIDS, in Maryland (301) 459-3388

The National Sudden Infant Death Foundation helps parents deal with the shock and grief of losing their babies to SIDS. The group provides information and counseling services. Foundation volunteers throughout the United States help connect parents who have lost babies through SIDS. A newsletter, *The Leaflet*, is published bimonthly and is free to all SIDS parents.

Parents of Murdered Children (POMC)
1739 Bella Vista
Cincinnati, OH 45237
(513) 242-8025

POMC puts families who have experienced the death of a murdered child in touch with one another. In chapters throughout the United States, parents can find support and be with others who will listen and understand.

Parents Without Partners
8807 Colesville Rd.
Silver Spring, MD 20910
(301) 588-9354

Parents Without Partners is an organization of custodial and noncustodial single parents. It promotes the study of the problems of single parenting and offers support for single parents.

Pregnancy and Infant Loss Center
1415 East Wayzata Blvd.
Wayzata, MN 55391
(612) 473-9372

This nonprofit organization offers families and professionals relevant information and counseling services and coordinates materials produced by other organizations.

Resolve Through Sharing
LaCrosse-Lutheran Hospital
1910 South Ave.
LaCrosse, WI 54601
(608) 785-0530, ext. 3675

This group provides information for professionals and for families who have lost babies through miscarriage, stillbirth, or newborn death.

The Samaritans/Safe Place
33 Chestnut St.
Providence, RI 02903
(401) 272-4044

For survivors of suicide victims, this group provides self-help support in resolving grief, guilt, and anger. The meetings allow bereaved survivors an opportunity to ventilate their feelings and talk about painful reminders.

Source of Help in Airing and Resolving Experiences (SHARE)
Saint Joseph's Health Center
300 First Capitol Dr.
St. Charles, MO 63301
(314) 947-5487

SHARE offers support in dealing with the grief of parents experiencing the death of a newborn, stillbirth, miscarriage, or ectopic pregnancy. A bimonthly newsletter written by parents and professionals provides information on national and international meetings as well as meetings of other support groups for bereaved parents.

References

Bordow, Joan (1982). *The Ultimate Loss: Coping with the Death of a Child.* New York: Beaufort Books.

Bridges, William (1980). *Transitions: Making Sense Out of Life's Changes.* Reading, MA: Addison-Wesley.

Clark, Martha Bittle (1987). *Are You Weeping with Me, God?* Nashville: Broadman Press.

Corr, Charles A.; Fuller, Helen; Barnickel, Carol Ann; and Corr, Donna M. (Eds.) (1991). *Sudden Infant Death Syndrome.* New York: Springer.

Cousins, Norman (1979). *Anatomy of an Illness.* New York: Bantam.

Davis, Deborah L. (1991). *Empty Cradle, Broken Heart: Surviving the Death of Your Baby.* Golden, CO: Fulcrum Publishing.

Donnelly, Katherine Fair (1982). *Recovering from the Loss of a Child.* New York: Macmillan.

Gibran, Kahlil (1923). *The Prophet.* New York: Knopf.

Hine, Virginia, and Foster, Steven (1979). *Rites of Passage for Our Time: A Guide for Creating Rituals.* Unpublished manuscript.

Ilse, Sherokee, and Burns, Linda Hammer (1985). *Miscarriage: A Shattered Dream.* Long Lake, MN: Wintergreen Press.

Klass, Dennis (1988). *Parental Grief: Solace and Resolution.* New York: Springer.

Lindbergh, Anne Morrow (1973). *Hour of Gold, Hour of Lead.* New York: Signet Books.

O'Neil, Nena, and O'Neil, George (1974). *Shifting Gears: Finding Security in a Changing World.* New York: Evans.

Rando, Therese A. (Ed.) (1986). *Parental Loss of a Child.* Champaign, IL: Research Press.

Redmond, Lula Moshoures (1989). *Surviving: When Someone You Love Was Murdered.* Clearwater, FL: Psychological Consultation and Education Services.

Sanders, Catherine M. (1989). *Grief: The Mourning After.* New York: Wiley.

Sanders, Catherine M. (1992). *Surviving Grief and Learning to Live Again.* New York: Wiley.

Schiff, Harriet Sarnoff (1977). *The Bereaved Parent.* New York: Crown.

Selye, Hans (1974). *Stress without Distress.* New York: Lippincott.

Stearns, Ann Kaiser (1984). *Living through Personal Loss.* New York: Ballantine.

Stillion, Judith M.; McDowell, Eugene E.; and May, Jacque H. (1989). *Suicide across the Life Span.* New York: Hemisphere Publishing.

Books About Codependency

Beattie, Melody (1987). *Codependent No More.* New York: Harper & Row.

Bradshaw, John (1980). *Homecoming: Reclaiming and Championing Your Inner Child.* New York: Bantam.

Friel, John, and Friel, Linda (1988). *The Secrets of Dysfunctional Families.* Deerfield Beach, FL: Health Communications.

Oliver-Diaz, Phillip, and O'Gorman, Patricia (1988). *12 Steps to Self-Parenting.* Deerfield Beach, FL: Health Communications.

Index

Abandonment
  fear of, 61, 83, 177
  and inner child, 55
  of murder victims, 107
  of siblings, 97–99
Abortion
  decisions for, 125, 127
  grief after, 70, 74
  guilt after, 52
Acceptance
  after loss, 38, 173, 215
  after suicide, 115
  of challenges, 196–197
  of death, 211
  during healing, 32
  of feelings, 52, 93, 212
  and forgiveness, 36, 178–180
  and growth, 193–194
  and humility, 198
  of imperfection, 55–56
  and letting go, 163
Accidents
  in adolescence, 2, 3–6, 12–13, 14,
    21, 51, 164
  and childhood death, 178
  as punishment, 34
Acquired Immune Deficiency Syn-
    drome (AIDS), 115–118
Adaptation
  to life after loss, 182–183
  to losing grandchildren, 186–187
  to new circumstances, 168, 203
Adolescents. See also Accidents;
    Children
  and AIDS, 116
  conflict with parents, 13–15, 51
  death by murder, 102–104
  death from violence, 102–103
  frequency of accidental death, 14
  and sibling grief, 98
  suicide rate for, 113
Adoption, 70, 131
Adrenaline, 28, 161. See also Illness;
    Immune System
Age of child, at death, 12
Alarm, state of, 21–22, 28
Alcohol
  death involving, 82
  in families, 65, 66, 81–82

and guilt, 52
and men, 88
and pregnancy, 140
in relationships, 126
Alienation, 15–16. See also Isolation
Ambivalence. See also Feelings
  about abortion, 126–127
  about guilt, 50–52
  about teenagers, 14
  and length of grief process, 16–17
  in marriage, 10
Ambulance crews, 5, 58
American Association of Suicidology
    (AAS), 227
Amniocentesis, 128
Anatomy of an Illness, 184
Anger
  after miscarriage, 120, 124–125
  after murder of child, 30, 105,
    107–109, 111
  at death of child, 14, 33–34,
    59–60, 90, 159
  at fate, 45
  at spiritual advice, 17
  at suicide victims, 114–115
  and awareness of loss, 24, 26, 213
  and blame, 77
  by men, 11, 27, 33–34, 56, 89–90, 92
  by women, 11, 56, 93, 123, 125, 131
  dangers of, 60
  displaced, 58–59
  and forgiveness, 178–180
  and guilt, 46
  letting go of, 55
  in marriage, 96
  and missing children, 39
  as safety valve, 57–58, 60
  and spiritual growth, 17–18, 60, 61
Anniversaries, 42, 49, 149–150
Anxiety, 26
Appreciation, 199–200
Asking for help, in grief, 211
"Automatic pilot," and shock, 23
Automobiles, 2, 12–13, 66
Awareness of loss, 24–28. See also
    Grief process; Phases in grief
  and reminders of child, 19, 25
  suggestions for dealing with,
    212–214

About the Author

Catherine M. Sanders, Ph.D., is a psychologist in clinical practice in Charlotte, North Carolina. In her work she specializes in helping those who have suffered a traumatic loss. She has done extensive research into the effects of bereavement on the individual and on the family constellation. Her work in the field of loss and grief dates back to 1968, when she began construction of the Grief Experience Inventory, a multidimensional instrument designed to measure intensities of grief in bereaved individuals. The GEI is now being used in the United States and abroad in research and clinical situations.

After completing her Ph.D. at the University of South Florida, Dr. Sanders founded and was director of the Loss and Bereavement Resource Center at the university, where she consulted, provided training programs for professionals, conducted research, and taught graduate courses in death and dying. She received both pre- and postdoctoral fellowships from the National Institute of Mental Health to study the effects of bereavement on adults. Her postdoctoral fellowship was done at Cushing Hospital in Framingham, Massachusetts, where she examined the effects of grief on the family constellation. She served on a national committee in Washington to develop a training program for hospice nurses. In her current research, Dr. Sanders is focusing on the processes and effects of grief following separation or divorce.

As psychological consultant to WBTV in Charlotte, Dr. Sanders appeared weekly to report on a variety of topics and to answer questions from the viewing audience. She has written extensively about bereavement and is author of *Grief: The Mourning After* (John Wiley & Sons, 1989), which the National Library Association recognized as the outstanding book in its field. Dr. Sanders also wrote *Surviving Grief and Learning to Live Again* (John Wiley & Sons, 1992). In 1990 the Association for Death Education and Counseling presented her with its annual award for outstanding contribution in the field of death-related counseling.